MY PADERNO VEGETABLE SPIRALIZER RECIPE BOOK

DELECTABLE AND SURPRISINGLY EASY PALEO, GLUTEN-FREE AND WEIGHT LOSS RECIPES!

(VOLUME 2, EDITION 2)

Written by

J.S. Amie

www.HealthyHappyFoodie.org

ISBN-13: 978-1500746339
ISBN-10: 1500746339

This book is for entertainment purposes. The publisher and author of this book are not responsible in any manner whatsoever for any adverse effects arising directly or indirectly as a result of the information provided in this book.

FULL COLOR PHOTOS AND RECIPES!

This book is special: it's a *digitally expanded* recipe book! In addition to the physical book you have in your hands, you can download and access a growing body of digital content—full color photos, videos, more detailed tips and instructions, and more delicious recipes—just by going online. It's already part of your purchase, so come and get it!

With a digital component to this book, you get the best of both worlds! A nice recipe book for easy access in the kitchen, plus the full and multidimensional experience that only online content can provide.

To access the digital part of this book, just go to
www.HealthyHappyFoodie.org/digital-paderno

WHAT'S IN THIS BOOK?

This book is the second book in a series of recipe books featuring "spiralized" and julienne-cut vegetables as substitutes for pasta and other traditional ingredients. When I purchased my first vegetable spiralizer, I was excited to try making zucchini noodles, also known as "zoodles." My first dish — zucchini spaghetti with fresh tomatoes, basil and garlic — was fun, creative, and delicious! I quickly found that zoodles were popular with my friends and family. Everyone seemed pleasantly surprised by the experience and enthusiastically asked for more!

But when I began looking for recipes to satisfy my family's cravings for more, I couldn't find any! There were a few recipes here and there in popular Gluten-free cookbooks, but the recipes were uninspired, and did not fully capture the variety of flavors, textures and uses for this revolutionary way of preparing vegetables.

Additionally, I found very little in the way of "how to" instructions and advice for using these handy kitchen tools. I noticed that many people were having difficulties choosing the right vegetables for optimum results. I also read complaints from people who wanted to know how to handle the cutters correctly and safely. Hint: if you use them correctly, they won't bite!

Eventually, after extensively experimenting with each of the most popular spiralizers (such as the Paderno Spiralizer, and the Veggetti), as well as various julienne peelers, I realized it was time to share my experience with others and hopefully inspire cooks everywhere to see for themselves how absolutely divine zoodles can be!

Who This Book Is For

Vegetable spiralizers were made to help people live healthier lives by replacing wheat in their diets while increasing the amount of vegetables they eat. Anyone who is trying to cut wheat out of his or her diet will immediately see the possibilities that open up when you have the ability to make your own delicious vegetable pasta substitutes.

The popular Paderno Spiralizer, Veggetti Spiral Vegetable Cutter and other spiralizers and julienne slicers are perfect for food lovers on any kind of regimen, including Gluten-Free, Paleo or weight-loss diets. This book will not only give you great recipes to utilize your new vegetable cutter, but it will show you how to use these utensils safely and efficiently.

TABLE OF CONTENTS

Chapter 5: Paleo Recipes

Chapter 6: Weight Loss Recipes

Chapter 7: Soups

Chapter 8: Bonus Section:

Keeping A Well-Stocked Pantry

WHERE TO START?

Use the list below to locate the recipes shown on the back cover. Each is delicious, fun to make, and an excellent starting point for your spiralizer adventure!

Chapter 1

SPIRALIZING TOOLS

Using the right tool for the job is—as any handyman/woman knows—the key to success; you don't use a hammer to tighten a screw. There are three kinds of vegetable slicers on the market, and all have strengths and weaknesses you should be aware of when making a choice. (Or buy all three and have options!)

The Veggetti Spiral Vegetable Slicer

Best for: quick set up, small quantities of noodles, small "footprint" on the counter, and traveling.

This inventive, hourglass-shaped kitchen utensil is easy to use, easy to clean, and lightweight enough to carry with you when you travel. If you can imagine a pencil sharpener large enough to accommodate a zucchini, then you've just imagined the Veggetti Spiral Vegetable Slicer and how it works.

As with anything in your kitchen that has a blade—blender, food processor, silverware drawer— the Veggetti can bite if you're not careful. The blades are extremely sharp, so you need to be alert while you're turning your vegetables into delicious, low-calorie spaghetti strands. Most mishaps occur when a hand slips while guiding the vegetable through the blades, or when someone sticks a finger into the blade during cleaning.

Keep in mind that very little force is necessary. All you need to do is gently twist your vegetables through, preferably using the Veggetti's cap to grip the vegetable while you're twisting it.

Here's how to use the Veggetti safely:

STEP 1: Leave the skin on the gripping end of the vegetable. This gives you a more solid and less slippery surface to grip while you're twisting the vegetable into the Veggetti.

Notes: For most vegetables—such as zucchinis, carrots, yellow squash—I simply grip the end of the vegetable with my hand. However, the Veggetti comes with a "cap" that has little spikes which help to grip slippery vegetables. I find that this cap works well for dense vegetables (carrots), but not for soft vegetables (zucchini). In my experience, the cap will shred the end of soft vegetables, making it even more difficult to push them through the Veggetti. Another option to get the last inch of goodness out of each vegetable, is to stab a fork into the vegetable instead of using your fingers or the cap.

STEP 2: the Veggetti cutter looks like an hourglass with two open ends. Each "funnel" has a different blade so that you can vary the type of vegetable pasta you get—spaghetti-type strands or wider, udon noodles. Choose the width of noodle you want and guide your vegetable into that blade.

> Notes: You'll quickly develop a preference for either the spaghetti or the udon noodle size for each vegetable. I love both, depending on the dish. Generally, I prefer the thinner spaghetti noodles for denser vegetables (carrots, beets, etc). For raw or lightly cooked dishes, I also prefer the thinner spaghetti noodles. However, the thicker udon noodles are great for soups, or dishes with thick sauces.

STEP 3: Once your vegetable is cleaned, scrubbed, or peeled, simply place the end you want to cut into the Veggetti and begin turning it, just as you would when sharpening a pencil. The "pasta" strands will begin appearing as soon as the turning starts. Discard the left over portion of the vegetable or save it for another use, like enriching soup.

> Notes: Keep your fingers away from the blades! The Veggetti is known to bite if you're not careful. The best way to keep your fingers safe is to make sure the part of the vegetable you're gripping is dry, unpeeled, and firm. Otherwise use the Veggetti's cap or use a fork to grip the vegetable while you're spiralizing it.

> For zucchini, I like to leave the stem on and use it as a grip while spiralizing. I find this to work so well that I never use the Veggetti's cap or a fork when spiralizing zucchini.

> For carrots, parsnips, yellow squash, and other vegetables shaped like cones, I like to hold the thin end while spiralizing the thick end so I can use more and waste less of the vegetable.

> For eggplant, I like to use the thicker cut because the thinner pasta strands are more fragile than the thicker pasta. Keep in mind that eggplant noodles are notoriously fragile and break easily.

One trick I've learned is to hold the Veggetti a little differently than shown in the manufacturer's instructions. The spiralizing process tends to produce a lot of excess "vegetable" matter and it can get a little messy, with bits of veggie goop falling out the opposite end of the Veggetti and into your plate. I like to cup that end of the Veggetti

with my left hand when I spiralize with my right hand. This allows me to catch the vegetable goop in my palm so I can discard it easily.

Best veggies to use with the Veggetti:

The Veggetti works best with vegetables that have a tubular shape like zucchini, or cone-like shape like a carrot. The vegetable needs to be able to fit into the blades, and you need to be able to turn the vegetable easily in order to produce nice pasta strands. Therefore, any irregular shaped vegetable, or any oversized or undersized vegetable will  not work very well. Use this tool for vegetables sized between 1-1/2" and 2-1/2" diameter. Anything smaller causes too much waste, and anything larger simply cannot fit!

- **Zucchini**—snip the nose off the zucchini, and use the stem on the other end as a handle to guide the vegetable through the cutter.
- **Yellow squash**—snip the nose off the squash, and hold the vegetable along the thin end (the stem end) so that the thicker part of the vegetable is turned into noodles and there's less waste.
- **Cucumbers**—snip the nose off, peel most of the skin but make sure to leave the skin on the gripping end so your hand doesn't slip!
- **Carrots, Turnips, and other similar roots**—cut ½" from the stem end (the thick end) and grip the thin end. This provides more noodle and less waste. Be careful to choose carrots that are not cracked, as cracks will cause short circles instead of long strands of pasta.
- **Sweet Potatoes, Yams, Potatoes, Beets**—if the potato or beet is large, you may need to cut it down to a size that can be handled by the Veggetti. Be VERY careful with these vegetables, they are slippery and can easily cause injury. I always use the Veggetti cap to grip these vegetables while spiralizing.

Worst veggies to use with the Veggetti:

- **Apples**—too large and too difficult to grip.
- **Eggplants**—too large, and the pasta strands can easily fall apart.
- Vegetables with irregular shapes.

The Paderno Spiralizer

Best for: large quantities of noodles, and greater variety of cuts and shreds. It takes more counter space and more time to set up than a Veggetti, but once it's set up, it works much faster

The Paderno Spiralizer is a hand-powered tool, which means it is neither battery-powered nor electrical. About the size of a counter-top mixer, it is safer than other hand-held vegetable spiralizers, such as the Veggetti, because the vegetable is inserted into the machine, and directed toward the cutting blades by the action of a turning crank—the cook's hands never get anywhere near the sharp surfaces.

The Paderno has three blades that produce three different types of noodles:

Thin Spaghetti-sized noodles

Thick udon/linguini-size noodles

Wide, flat lasagna noodles—the width depending on the diameter of the vegetable/fruit being cut. This blade also shreds certain vegetables like cabbage, which makes it useful for quickly making slaws and salads.

Here's how to use the Paderno safely:

STEP 1: Make certain the machine is firmly "seated" on the counter and that all four suction cups are "engaged." You do this by simply pushing down on the Paderno's legs. Put your body into it! If you don't set the suction cups, as soon as you start using the machine, it will slide right off the counter. To release the suction, simply break the seal by pushing a finger under the suction cups.

STEP 2: Select the appropriate blade depending on how you want to process your vegetable. There are three blades provided with this slicer (thin, thick, and wide).

STEP 3: Sandwich the vegetable to be spiralized or shredded into the machine, holding it in place with the prongs. Be careful to center the vegetable against the blade as well as you can, otherwise it will be more difficult to spiralize.

STEP 4: With your left hand, push the lever forward toward the blade, while turning the crank with your right hand to cut the vegetable. Keep firm pressure against the blade to produce the best results. Do not push on the crank as that might break it. To get shorter "pasta" pieces, cut a groove in the vegetable so that when the "spirals" are sliced off, they are automatically cut, creating the smaller (short) pasta shapes.

Notes: I've found that dense vegetables (such as beets and jicama) can be difficult to successfully spiralize. The Paderno's blades don't always cut deeply enough to slice all the way through, producing full-width noodles that look scored instead of cut. The reason is because dense vegetables require more force to keep them lined up correctly on the blades. But applying too much force to the Paderno can break it. Unfortunately, I haven't found a reliable way to handle this problem other than to grip the lever closer to its hinge and apply more pressure while turning the crank very carefully.

Quirks: Some vegetables may need to be trimmed a bit so that it will easily fit into the center blade.

With some vegetables you'll need to cut a bit off the vegetable so that the crank end will grip it properly. Simply slice off a piece to flatten the end of the vegetable and push the flat end into the prongs to secure it. (With apples, you don't need to do anything except stick the fruit on the crank and start turning.)

Best veggies to use with the Paderno Spiralizer:

The Paderno is particularly good with soft and less dense vegetables and can easily handle larger vegetables that have a diameter of up to 5 inches.

- **Apples**–particularly nice when cut into the "udon" size
- **Cabbages**–great for shredding.
- **Zucchini**–terrific for large zucchini.
- **Yellow Squash**–also terrific if the squash is large enough.
- **Onions**–for fast shredding.
- **Larger vegetables** (up to 5 inches in diameter)

Worst veggies to use with the Paderno spiralizer

- **Beets**–are difficult for the Paderno to slice because they are so dense and tough. Turn the crank slowly for best results. And always peel the beet before spiralizing.
- **Carrots, Turnips, etc**–unless you can find huge carrots or turnips, most carrots are simply too small in diameter to be spiralized by the Paderno. Large carrots also have a tendency to crack on the Paderno. Use a Veggetti or Julienne slicer instead.
- **Small zucchini**–if your zucchini is less than 1-1/2" in diameter, it will produce more waste than noodles in the Paderno. Use a Veggetti or Julienne slicer instead.

The Julienne Slicer and Mandoline

Best for: precision slicing, matchstick cuts, difficult vegetables and fruit, portability.

This is the 21st century version of the cooking tool first known as the "mandoline." It is a low-tech tool with no moving parts, just a set of wicked sharp blades that create different sizes and styles of vegetable slices, including crinkle-cut vegetables for "fries."

Best for: nice flat "lasagna" ribbons ranging from thick to ultra-thin, and julienne-cut vegetables

While it is a low-tech gadget, it has been maximized to make it easy to adjust thicknesses while slicing allowing for cuts from paper-thin to thick. There is a purpose-built julienne blade included that will allow for perfect "matchstick" cuts as well. Although the spiralizer-style cutters can create julienne strips, the mandoline is a fast alternative to chopping by hand and is also easier to clean than either the Veggetti or the Paderno style spiralizers.

Best veggies to use with a Mandoline / Julienne Slicer: any!

How To Clean Your Spiralizer

The number one easiest way to clean each of these wonderful spiralizing tools is to wash them under running water immediately after use. If you wash immediately after using, then any vegetable matter will easily slough off of the tool and its blades. Warm soapy water is more effective as it softens the vegetable matter even more. Simply run water over the blades, and use your kitchen brush if needed, then put the tool on your drying rack. The entire process takes 30 seconds.

If you don't clean your spiralizer right away, then you'll have some extra work to do. The entire Veggetti is dishwasher-proof, as are the blades on the Paderno, so for the most part, all you need to do is throw the appliance in the dishwasher and hit "go." But there are times when particles of vegetable matter will cling to the blades. When that happens, there are two easy ways to clean out the debris without putting your fingers at risk.

One method is to use hot water with the sink power sprayer to force the particles out. The second is to use a clean toothbrush to gently scrub the sharp surfaces. (Buy them by the handful at the dollar store and keep a couple in your utensil drawer. You'll be amazed at how useful they'll be.)

For Julienne slicers of any type, hand-washing is recommended. Use the power-rinse at your sink and run hot water through the device to remove any food debris. Wash immediately after use if cutting zucchini or beets, which can leave stains.

Chapter 2

ALL ABOUT VEGETABLES

Not all vegetables and fruits work with each type of cutter. Each different type of vegetable cutter has its pros, cons, and quirks. For example, a tomato can be sliced by a mandolin-type slicer, but it would turn to mush in a Veggetti or Paderno-style spiralizer. Nor can you spiralize vegetables and fruits with pits (avocados, stone fruits).

You can't spiralize vegetables that are smaller than 1 ½ inches in diameter. That category would include asparagus, green beans, and Chinese long beans. Very soft ingredients—like bananas—also don't work well in a spiralizer-type cutter, and neither will fruits like kiwi and watermelon that are mostly water. But again, the mandolin-style slicers work fine for these vegetables or fruits.

What Are The Best Vegetables (and Fruits) To Spiralize?

Here is a list of vegetables and fruits which I've found to spiralize well:

Apples

Nutrition: Apples are nutrient filled and fiber rich. A medium apple has approximately 115 calories and a low glycemic index (GI) number of 37. They also provide, among other vitamins and minerals, 28% of the RDA of vitamin C.

Best way to spiralize: Apples range from tart to super sweet and any of the three basic kinds of vegetable cutter will work well with them. For best results, use firm apples without any soft spots. Leave the peel on to add a bit of color to the noodles.

Cooking tips: best eaten raw or baked.

Beets

Nutrition: These low-calorie, high-fiber and zero cholesterol roots contain antioxidant vitamins A and C, which help protect against cardiovascular disease and reduce the risk of stroke. They also contain minerals such as iron, potassium, copper, magnesium, and manganese—all of which are important in maintaining optimum health of systems.

Best way to spiralize: Beets are dense, hard vegetables and can be difficult to spiralize with a Paderno. I recommend using either a Julienne slicer or a Veggetti cutter. You may need to cut the beet down to less than 2-1/2" diameter, and slightly shape it with a knife before spiralizing it with the Veggetti.

Cooking tips: Beets can be eaten raw, or cooked. Let the recipe or your own inspiration guide you.

Bell peppers

Nutrition: Bell peppers of any color are rich sources of vitamin C and carotenoids, powerful antioxidants that have been shown to significantly reduce the likelihood of lung cancer.

Best way to spiralize: They work best with the mandoline-type slicers, whose precise cuts make for a professional presentation in dishes as diverse as sukiyaki and salads.

Cooking tips: They can be eaten raw or cooked.

Broccoli

Nutrition: Broccoli is one of the cancer-fighting cruciferous vegetables, and contains more vitamin C than an orange.

Best way to spiralize: The fibrous stalks are difficult to slice in either a Veggetti or Paderno—they're too irregularly shaped for the Veggetti and they split on the Paderno. However, the mandolin-style cutters will provide neat julienne slices faster and more uniformly than using a chef's knife will.

Cooking tips: The fibrous stalks of broccoli are perfect for short veggie pasta but they should be blanched before eating to cut down on the strong taste.

Cabbage

Nutrition: Like broccoli, cabbage belongs to the cruciferous vegetable family. (Other members include Brussels sprouts, bok choy, and cresses. All varieties of cabbage contain sinigrin, an anti-cancer nutrient but Savoy cabbage is a particularly good source.

Best way to spiralize: Cabbage cannot be cut into pasta strands, but it shreds very well on the Paderno. You can vary the size of the shreds by choosing different Paderno blades. If using a Paderno slicer to shred cabbage for slaws or stir-fries, it's best to use a small head.

Cooking tips: It can be eaten raw, but steaming the vegetable makes it particularly effective for lowering cholesterol.

Cauliflower

Nutrition: Cauliflower is nutritionally dense—low in carbohydrates but high in fiber, folate (necessary for nerve health and emotional well-being), and antioxidant vitamin C. It is also high in vitamin K, which is essential for effective blood clotting. Cauliflower contains phytochemicals which have been shown to protect against various kinds of cancer.

Best way to spiralize: The "wide" blade of the Paderno slicer is perfect for turning cauliflower into

"rice" or "couscous." If a finer grain is desired, you can also process it further in a food processor.

Cooking tips: Cauliflower should be cooked before eating. Because the texture of cauliflower rice is important, I recommend following the recipe's cooking instructions.

Carrots

Nutrition: A medium sized carrot has only 52 calories, 12 grams of carbohydrate, 4 grams of fiber and is one of the best natural sources of vitamin A. Carrots also contain iron, B6 and other B vitamins, manganese, vitamins E, K and C, along with phosphorus, choline, potassium and calcium. Carrots are naturally sweet.

Best way to spiralize: Carrots are often a little small for the Paderno, so they are best spiralized in a Veggetti cutter, or a mandoline-style slicer for uniform julienne cuts.

Cooking tips: Eat them raw (thin carrot noodles are delicious raw), warm them with sauce or in soup, or cook them briefly in boiling water.

Celeriac

Nutrition: Touted as an underrated vegetable by Epicurious and Martha Stewart, Celeriac is also known as "celery root." This root vegetable looks like a turnip and tastes much like the better known vegetable "celery." Unlike most other root vegetables, celeriac contains almost no starch. The vegetable contains large amounts of vitamin K (important for blood clotting), as well as C and B vitamins.

Best way to spiralize: It works well in all three types of vegetable slicers.

Cooking tips: It can be eaten raw or cooked, and is often mashed as a substitute for potatoes on weight-loss diets.

Chayote Squash

Nutrition: Chayote squash generally look like big green pears. It is high in potassium and low in sodium.

Best way to spiralize: All three slices can be used on this vegetable, but it has to be cut into smaller pieces for the Veggetti.

Cooking tips: It can be eaten raw or cooked and its extremely mild flavor makes it perfect for pasta dishes where a more assertively flavored noodle (like broccoli) would overpower the taste.

Citrus Fruit (only for the mandolin-type slicer)

All you'll get is pulpy juice if you try to spiralize citrus fruit with a Paderno or Veggetti slicer. But a mandolin-style slicer is the perfect tool for shaving precise slices on everything from a tiny kumquat to a ruby red grapefruit. Whether the slices are being used as an essential ingredient—in something like a tomato quiche or a pitcher of sangria—or a garnish for a platter of poached salmon, the citrus fruit adds more than a spark of taste,

Cucumber

Nutrition: Cucumbers are related to the squash family and contain high amounts of vitamin K as well as antioxidant and anti-inflammatory substances. They are most often enjoyed as an ingredient in soups or salads.

Best way to spiralize: They work well with all spiralizers slicers. The Veggetti and Paderno produce easy noodles, while the mandoline-style slicers produce lovely cucumber salad slices.

Cooking tips: Cucumbers can be eaten raw or cooked, peeled or intact.

Eggplant

Nutrition: Eggplant contains important phytonutrients and antioxidants like nasunin, which protects the circulatory system.

Best way to spiralize: Eggplant is difficult to spiralize with a Veggetti, but the wide, flat eggplant "lasagna noodles' made with a Paderno slicer or a mandoline slicer make an excellent base for traditional recipes like moussaka and lasagna.

Cooking tips: Eggplant should not be eaten raw. Roasting is particularly delicious way of cooking eggplant. Some recipes are better if you salt the raw eggplant and let the water drain out prior to cooking.

Jerusalem artichoke

Nutrition: Also known as "sunchoke" or "sunroot," the Jerusalem artichoke is actually a species of sunflower. It is often used as a substitute for potatoes because of its satisfyingly starchy texture. It is a rich source of the B vitamin thiamine, providing 20 percent of the RDA.

Best way to spiralize: Because of its size, it works well with the Paderno and mandoline-style slicers.

Cooking tips: They can be eaten raw but may cause "gas" if eaten in that state.

Jicama

Nutrition: Also known as "yambean," jicama is a rich source of the antioxidant vitamin C and nerve-protecting B vitamins as well as several trace minerals including potassium, which protects against heart disease. Other nutrients found in jicama are anti-inflammatory and anti-viral.

Best way to spiralize: Jicama is too large to spiralize in a Veggetti unless you cut it down to manageable size. It is also quite dense, which requires extra care to spiralize in a Paderno. A Julienne slicer works particularly well with jicama.

Cooking tips: It can be eaten raw and is often sold as a street snack in Mexico, sprinkled with lime juice and chili powder.

Leeks

Nutrition: Leeks are an extremely healthy food, with almost 30% of the RDA for vitamin K as well as 13% of the RDA for manganese, which is important for reproductive health.

Best way to spiralize: Leeks make lovely ribbons of flat pasta that work well in soups, salads, and pasta dishes. They can be spiralized, Paderno-ized, and sliced with a mandoline.

Cooking tips: Like other members of the allium family, leeks can be eaten raw, but the are best when cooked to al dente perfection. My favorite way of serving any size or shape of leek is blanched with a sprinkle of olive oil and French sea salt.

Onion

Nutrition: Onions are a member of the "allium family," along with garlic, shallots, and leeks, and like its fellow family members, it is rich in flavonoids, including quercetin,

which has antioxidant and anti-inflammatory properties that protect the circulatory system and male reproductive system.

Best way to spiralize: The Paderno slicer shreds onions in seconds with no tears, but mandoline-style slicers are also useful for cutting uniform slices. (Onion rings anyone?)

Parsnip

Nutrition: Parsnips are a surprisingly sweet root vegetable and contain almost as much sugar as the average banana. In addition to anti-inflammatory, anti-fungal, and anti-cancer properties, parsnips are good sources of folate, vitamin C, and vitamins K and E.

Best way to spiralize: Like carrots, parsnips work best in the Veggetti or mandoline-style cutters unless they're very large (over two inches in diameter), in which case a Paderno works brilliantly.

Cooking tips: Baking and roasting are my preferred ways to cook Parsnips.

Pear

Slicing up a pears for desserts like clafouti or pie is a lot faster using either the Veggetti or Paderno slicer. There's no need to peel the fruit, simply wash and dry well before beginning the slicing process. (Pear skins have three to four times the nutrient value of the rest of the fruit, and those nutrients include antioxidants, anti-inflammatory and anti-cancer substances.) Extra bonus for diabetics—the flavonoids in pears can improve insulin sensitivity.

Plantain

Nutrition: Green plantains are starchy but low in sugar (as long as you don't fry them). Plantains are good sources of copper, manganese, potassium, and magnesium, as well as vitamins A and B-6, which protects against stroke and other cardiovascular events. For best results use the straightest and firmest plantains you can find.

Best way to spiralize: Unlike their botanical cousins bananas, plantains are firm enough to stand up to any kind of veggie cutter.

Cooking tips: Plantains need to be cooked before eating. They can be pan-fried, grilled and baked.

Potatoes

Nutrition: While potatoes have a bad rep, a medium-sized potato only contains about 100 calories

while delivering significant amounts of the antioxidant vitamins A and C, B6 and other B vitamins, as well as bone-building calcium and magnesium, potassium, and phosphorus.

Best way to spiralize: If the potato is small enough, both thin and thick blades on a Veggetti spiralizer works well. For large potatoes or large quantities, use a Paderno and choose the blade that best fits the recipe.

Cooking tips: Always cook potatoes before eating. Potato noodles can fall apart when boiled.

Pumpkin

Nutrition: Pumpkin can be substituted for any other type of squash. Pumpkin noodles are mildly flavored and colorful. Pumpkin "fries" are a low-calorie, low cholesterol, and low sodium substitute for traditional fries and they deliver hefty doses of vitamins A, C, and E, as well as B vitamins, including folic acid, and potassium, copper, and manganese.

Best way to spiralize: Pumpkin needs to be cut down before it can be spiralized. As long as you cut the pumpkin to a somewhat regular shape, it can be spiralized by a Veggetti or Paderno. However, because of the extra effort involved in cutting pumpkin to an appropriate shape for spiralizing, I prefer to use a julienne slicer for quick pumpkin noodles or matchsticks.

Cooking tips: Baking and roasting are preferred ways to cook pumpkin noodles, but check the recipe for specifics.

Radishes

Nutrition: Radishes are low-carb, low-calorie cancer fighters filled with immune-boosting vitamin C as well as vitamin K and B complex vitamins. Their mineral content (potassium, calcium, manganese, iron, phosphorus, zinc, and copper) help promote healthy bones and support optimum health.

Best way to spiralize: Because radishes are so small, they're difficult to spiralize with either Veggetti or Paderno slicers. However a julienne slicer can easily produce beautifully thin slices or matchsticks.

Cooking tips: Radishes are excellent raw.

Squash

Nutrition: All varieties of squash are low-calorie, low-carb, cholesterol-free, and high in fiber. They

are also high in the antioxidant vitamins A and C, and contain significant amounts of niacin, folic acid, potassium, and iron. Squashes are anti-inflammatory and contain no fat.

Best way to spiralize: Yellow squash is very easy to spiralize with either Veggetti, Paderno or julienne slicers. Other squashes can require cutting with a knife prior to spiralizing. My strong preference is to use yellow squash when possible, as the results are consistently wonderful with this commonly available squash.

Cooking tips: If it is fresh, yellow squash is sweet and delicious raw. However, it quickly develops a bitter taste when it is no longer fresh. Cook yellow squash lightly, or it will turn mushy and lose its wonderful texture and flavor. My preferred way to prepare squash is blanched with a little olive oil and sea salt.

Sweet Potato

Nutrition: The sweet potato is rich in antioxidants like beta-carotene and has a lower glycemic index (70) compared to a white potato (111).

Best way to spiralize: Sweet potatoes are hard, dense vegetables that can be difficult to spiralize. If less than 2-1/2" in diameter, try spiralizing with a Veggetti. Make sure to peel the part you want to spiralize, and leave the peel on the part you're holding. For a Paderno, peel it and cut both ends, and carefully spiralize with either blade. Sweet potatoes make excellent noodles and julienne-sliced "fries."

Cooking tips: Sweet potatoes should not be eaten raw. Boiling the noodles too long can cause them to fall apart.

Tomatoes

You can't spiralize tomatoes but you can use a handheld mandoline like the Microplane to slice them paper thin. Tomatoes can be eaten raw or cooked. Tomatoes are botanically fruit and their juicy flesh is a rich source of lycopene, a nutrient that can—among other things—limit and repair sun damage on skin.

Turnip

Nutrition: Turnips are an excellent source of anti-oxidants, minerals, vitamins and dietary fiber. They provide a healthy dose of vitamin C while containing only 28 calories per 100g.

Best way to spiralize: Like beets and rutabaga, turnips are hard and dense, which makes them difficult to spiralize. Try spiralizing in a Veggetti, taking care not to slip and cut your fingers. If the turnip is large enough, a Paderno may be used. As with the other dense vegetables, a julienne slicer may be a better tool to use.

Yam

Nutrition: Vitamin-rich yams are often mistaken for sweet potatoes but they are in fact, a completely different species of plant, a relative to flowers and grasses native to North Africa.

Best way to spiralize: They are large, dense vegetables and may be difficult for the Paderno to process. The Veggetti can spiralize them easily if the vegetable is cut into slices that will fit into the cutter. A julienne slicer can also work well.

Cooking tips: Yams should be peeled and cooked before eating as they contain toxins.

Zucchini

Nutrition: Zucchini is so popular as a vegetable alternative to wheat and rice pasta that it the green noodles are now called "zoodles." Zucchini is high in the antioxidant vitamins A and C, as well as Folate (critical for nerve health) and other B vitamins, as well as vitamin K. Low in sodium and cholesterol, Zucchini is a low-calorie source of dietary fiber and the minerals Phosphorus, Copper, Magnesium, Potassium, and Manganese.

Best way to spiralize: Zucchinis work very well with the Veggetti and mandoline-style slicers. If using the Paderno, choose fat, straight zucchini for best results.

Cooking tips: Fresh zucchini can be eaten raw, peeled or unpeeled. Often, if the recipe is a hot dish, simply mixing the raw zucchini noodles with the hot ingredients will "cook" the zucchini noodles enough to be perfectly and enjoyably "al dente." If you prefer your zucchini noodles to be cooked longer, then I recommend blanching for a few minutes and removing the cooked noodles from the pot to prevent overcooking.

How To Prepare and Cook Your Vegetable "Pasta"

Cooking your vegetable pasta is even easier than cooking traditional pasta! Here's how:

RAW

Most of the pasta you make from fruits and vegetables can be eaten raw. The exceptions are potatoes, sweet potatoes, and eggplant. Raw sweet potato contains an enzyme inhibitor that blocks the digestion of protein. Raw potatoes absorb bacteria from the soil and water (listeria, E. coli, and salmonella). They should be cooked before eating to destroy the bacteria. Raw eggplant contains a substance that inhibits the absorption of calcium and can also cause neurological and digestive problems.

Note: For most thin noodles made with soft vegetables (zucchini, yellow squash), mixing the warm or piping hot sauce with the raw noodles "cooks" them to just the desired "al dente" firmness.

WARMED

Warm the pasta strands by microwaving them for a few seconds in a microwave-safe bowl or by quickly "blanching" them in hot water before serving. (To blanch, bring a large pot of water to a boil. When the water is boiling, drop the noodles in and continue to heat for anywhere from 30 seconds to 10 minutes, depending on the vegetable. (Soft vegetables like zucchini or yellow squash take about 30 seconds; carrots take several minutes, beets can take as long as 10 minutes.)

BOILED

You will not need to "boil" your vegetable pasta unless you like the texture soft, bordering on mushy. Some vegetable pasta~white potatoes for instance~will simply fall apart after being boiled. An alternative cooking method would be "steaming," where the

vegetable pasta is put in a wire steaming basket and cooked over boiling water without actually being immersed in it.

TIP: if you undercook the pasta just a little, then drizzle with virgin olive oil, you'll never want to cook it any other way.

SAUTÉED

This is a simple technique for cooking the pasta and other ingredients quickly. The ingredients are placed in a pan—either a saucepan or a skillet—with a little fat or oil and cooked over high heat. The trick with this method is to stir often to prevent the ingredients from burning.

STIR-FRIED

Stir-frying is a quick-cooking method that requires very little fat. The secret to successful stir-fries is pre-prep. All the ingredients should be chopped or cut as needed so that everything will cook quickly. Woks are purpose-built for stir-frying, but any large, heavy skillet will do as well.

Here's a quick primer on how to stir fry:

- Make sure your ingredients are dry.
- Heat the oil over high heat, then add the aromatic ingredients (garlic, chilis, onions) and spices to the oil before adding any other ingredients. This allows the flavors to infuse the oil.
- Add the rest of the ingredients, being careful not to overcrowd the pan. If necessary cook in small batches.
- As with sautéing, you need to pay attention to the process; stir-frying is done over high heat and the ingredients can easily burn.

BAKED

Pasta in traditional dishes like mac and cheese has to be boiled first before being combined with the cheese sauce and baked. With vegetable noodles, you can simply add the raw noodles to the ingredients—they'll cook while the dish is baking, thus saving you a step. Keep in mind that vegetable noodles cook much more quickly than wheat pasta, therefore your baking times will be considerably shorter than usual.

How Much "Pasta" Will It Make?

For most traditional pasta recipes, the default ingredient is 1 pound of pasta, which yields 4 cups of cooked pasta. In the following recipes, 4 cups of vegetable spaghetti will be the standard ingredient. To get 4 cups of vegetable pasta from your veggies use the following guide. Equivalents are approximate depending on the size of the vegetable.

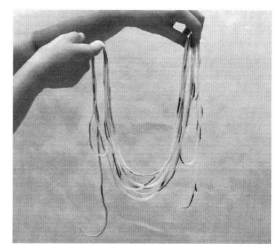

- **Beets** — 8 medium beets, trimmed = 4 cups beat pasta
- **Broccoli** — 6-8 trimmed broccoli stalks = 4 cups broccoli pasta
- **Carrot** — 8 medium carrots = 4 cups carrot pasta
- **Cauliflower** — 1 head of trimmed cauliflower = 4 cups cauliflower "rice"
- **Cucumbers** — 3-4 medium cucumbers = 4 cups cucumber pasta
- **Jicama** — 2 whole jicamas = 4 cups jicama pasta.
- **Potato** — 6 medium potatoes = 4 cups potato pasta
- **Radish** — 2 Daikon radishes = 4 cups radish pasta
- **Squash** — 4-6 yellow squash = 4 cups squash pasta
- **Sweet Potato** — 3 medium sweet potatoes = 4 cups sweet potato pasta
- **Zucchini** — 3-4 whole zucchini = 4 cups zucchini pasta

How To Store Leftover Vegetable Pasta

Leftover veggie noodles must be refrigerated, preferably in a container (glass or plastic) with an air-tight seal in the coldest part of the fridge. If the noodles have been cooked, or mixed with other hot ingredients, you can store them for up to 2 days. If the noodles are raw, they should be used within 24 hours. If you want to prevent discoloration, squeeze a little lemon juice over the raw pasta before storing.

Chapter 3

INGREDIENTS, TERMS & DIETS

"You don't have to cook fancy or complicated masterpieces - just good food from fresh ingredients."

— Julia Child

A Note On Ingredients

Unless otherwise noted, when a recipe calls for the following ingredients, you should use:

- **Brown sugar**—light brown sugar
- **Butter**—"sweet" (unsalted) butter
- **Chicken, beef, or vegetable stock**—low-sodium
- **Olive oil**—extra-virgin
- **Salt**—sea salt
- **Soy sauce**—low sodium, tamari-style
- **Sugar**—white, granulated
- **Yogurt**—unflavored, unsweetened, Greek-style

Prep Terms

Julienne—food cut into long, thin strips. "Shoestring fries" are julienned potatoes.

Matchstick—this is a thicker, more squared-off cut than a julienne and can range from thin (1/16th of an inch) to a 1/3 inch cut known in French as a batonnet cut.

Spiralized—this refers to vegetables or fruits cut into strands or spirals by using a Veggetti or Paderno slicer.

Rice or Couscous—refers to the small rice-like grains made by slicing Cauliflower head with a Veggetti or Paderno slicer. Try using the thick blade to make "rice" and the thin blade to make "couscous."

Pasta Terms

The spiralizer-type vegetable cutters used for this book create several different kinds of vegetable pasta, all of which are used in the recipes.

- **Spaghetti** (also interchangeable with Angel Hair)—refers to the long strands cut by the thin blades on either the Veggetti or the Paderno slicers.

- **Udon** (interchangeable with Linguini)—refers to the long strands cut by the thick blades on either the Veggetti or the Paderno slicers.
- **Flat**—refers to the long strands cut by the wide blade on the Paderno slicer, or the flat blade of a julienne slicer.
- **Spaghetti Circles**—the short, circular strands cut by scoring one side of a vegetable and slicing it with the thin blades on either the Veggetti or the Paderno slicers.
- **Udon Circles**—the short, circular strands cut by scoring one side of a vegetable and slicing it with the thick blades on either the Veggetti or the Paderno slicers.
- **Flat Circles**—the short, circular strands cut by scoring one side of a vegetable and slicing it the wide blade on the Paderno slicer.
- **Spaghetti Semicircles**—the short, semicircular strands cut by scoring both sides of a vegetable and slicing it with the thin blades on either the Veggetti or the Paderno slicers.
- **Udon Semicircles**—the short, semicircular strands cut by scoring both sides of a vegetable and slicing it with the thick blades on either the Veggetti or the Paderno slicers.
- **Flat Semicircles**—the short, semicircular strands cut by scoring both sides of a vegetable and slicing it the wide blade on the Paderno slicer.

Dietary Considerations

Gluten-Free (GF)

"Gluten "is the name given to several proteins found in cereal grains (wheat, barley, and rye are the biggest offenders, but it's also found in spelt and triticale, among other sources). Gluten makes dough more elastic, and is hidden in many foods under a variety of innocent-sounding ingredients. (For a full list of these gluten-containing ingredients, consult WebMD: http://www.webmd.com/diet/features/hidden-sources-of-gluten).

A growing body of research suggests that eating wheat — even in its whole form — contributes to a variety of health problems ranging from digestive disorders (Celiac disease, "leaky gut" syndrome) to obesity (what belly) and diabetes. There's even persuasive evidence that links wheat consumption to cognitive disorders ("grain brain").

Substituting fresh vegetable pasta for traditional wheat pasta is one small change that can result in huge benefits. Not only is eating "veggie pasta" a painless way to introduce more vegetables into any diet—always a good thing—but the increased fiber intake can help "reset" the body's metabolism, normalizing blood sugar, and replenishing depleted stocks of antioxidant vitamins and minerals, resulting in increased immune health.

For more information about gluten, contact The Celiac Disease Foundation http://celiac.org/live-gluten-free/glutenfreediet/what-is-gluten/

Glycemic Index (GI)

GI measures the impact a food has on the eater's blood sugar level. The scale basically ranges from 0-100, with 100 being the glycemic index of a slice of white bread. Diabetics and others with blood sugar issues are encouraged to eat low on the glycemic index, avoiding simple carbohydrates that metabolize into sugar quickly.

Glycemic Load (GL)

GL is a refinement of the measurement of glycemic index and takes into account the total makeup of a food, and not just its carbohydrates, as well as the portion size. Anything with a glycemic load under 10 is considered low glycemic. (Apples have a GL of 6; grapefruit is upper-low at 3.) A serving of Kraft macaroni and cheese comes in at a whopping GL of 32. Even adding in the milk and cheese to veggie noodle version, you'll still come out ahead, since the GL of a 4-oz. serving of zucchini is only 2.

Paleo

The Paleo Diet (aka "the Caveman Diet") is a back-to-basics food movement that focuses on the ingredients that were available to our caveman ancestors. That means no grains (cavemen were hunters, not farmers), no dairy and no sugar—the trifecta of ingredients responsible for the epidemic of obesity and the explosion of diabetes worldwide.

The Paleo diet also eliminates processed foods, including condiments like soy sauce, ketchup, and mustard, and all fats that are not plant-based. It's a very "clean" way of eating and ordinary pasta has no place on the Paleo plate. Veggie pasta, though, is wholeheartedly allowed.

Weight-Loss

Both Gluten-free and Paleo diets emphasize protein and "good carbs" and eliminate or limit sweets and grains. That's a good start for any weight-loss program. To lose weight you must do one of two things—eat less or exercise more, preferably both. But as any veteran dieter knows, not all calories are created equal. A cup of broccoli with humus will fill you up faster than a cup of chocolate pudding (which has triple the calories) will.

The recipes in this book are based on fresh veggie pastas made with the spiralizer and veggie cutters on the market today.

Salt

A special note about salt: the less the better, no matter what dietary plan you follow. A high-sodium intake stresses your kidneys, contributes to high blood-pressure, osteoporosis, diabetes, and water retention.

In general, all of the recipes in this book were created with an eye to lightening the sodium load. And really, any recipe that includes a high-salt ingredient like bacon, anchovies, or feta cheese really does not need additional salt. Try the recipes as is and you will be pleasantly surprised by how strongly flavored and delicious your food can be, even without a couple sprinkles of salt.

Chapter 4

GLUTEN-FREE RECIPES

A growing body of research suggests that eating grains — even in their whole forms — contributes to a variety of health problems ranging from digestive disorders (Celiac disease, "leaky gut" syndrome) to obesity and diabetes. Your vegetable slicer is a godsend for people with gluten-sensitivity because using it to make vegetable "spaghetti" makes it possible to enjoy (among other things) Italian food again.

rosemary pork ragout with sweet potato pasta

This pork ragout is delicious served with any type of pasta. However, the spiralized sweet potato pasta takes it up another notch, combining deep rosemary and pork flavors with the starchy sweetness of sweet potato. Guaranteed to transform a cold evening into a delight one.

prep time 3.5 h	calories 708	sodium 431 mg	dietary fiber 18.3 g
serves 4	total fat 12.9 g	total carbs 99.3 g	protein 48.4 g

method

SAUCE

1. Heat the olive oil in a heavy skillet and sear the pork roast on all sides.
2. Remove the meat from the pan and set aside.
3. Combine the garlic, onion and chopped rosemary and sauté in the remaining olive oil until the onion is translucent.
4. Combine the rosemary mixture with the meat in a large saucepan.
5. Pour in the crushed tomatoes, juice and all.
6. Add the seared pork loin.
7. Bring the liquid to a boil, then cover and reduce heat.
8. Simmer until the pork begins to fall apart (about 3 hours).
9. Remove the cooked meat from the liquid and let cool slightly.
10. Shred the meat and return to the pot, simmering another five minutes until everything has warmed up again.

"PASTA"

1. Use your vegetable spiralizer to create thick pasta strands from the sweet potatoes. Prepare or cook according to your preference. (Don't overcook or they'll get mushy).
2. Pour the Ragout over the pasta and garnish with additional rosemary sprigs if desired.

Serve immediately.

Note: The leftover ragout makes an excellent variation on the "Sloppy Joe" sandwich filling. A good gluten-free bun option is Udi's Gluten-Free hamburger buns.

ingredients

"PASTA"

4-6 sweet potatoes, peeled (with ends sliced off)

SAUCE

1 large yellow onion, roughly chopped

1 2-pound pork roast

3 sprigs fresh rosemary, chopped (or 3 tsp. dried rosemary)

2 large garlic cloves, minced

1 large (35-ounce) can crushed tomatoes (no salt)

Dash freshly ground black pepper

3 Tbsp. olive oil

vegetable fried "rice"

This is a quickie version of the traditional recipe, which often includes slices of an omelet. Make the "rice" by spiralizing the head of a cauliflower (not the stalk). If you want finer "grains", try pulsing the spiralized cauliflower in a food processor.

prep time 15 m	calories 308	sodium 305 mg	dietary fiber 12.6 g
serves 2	total fat 12.6 g	total carbs 41.0 g	protein 12.9 g

ingredients

"RICE"

2 cups Cauliflower heads

MAIN INGREDIENTS

2 green onions, chopped (use entire onion)

1 cup frozen or fresh snow peas

½ cup frozen corn

1 small green pepper, diced

1 small carrot, diced

1 ½ Tamari (or low-sodium soy sauce)

2 tsp. grated ginger

2-3 minced garlic cloves

¼ tsp. cayenne pepper

½ cup raw, unsalted sliced almonds

method

1. Heat a wok or heavy frying pan until very hot. Add oil and stir-fry the sliced almonds for 15 seconds.

2. Add the vegetables and stir-fry for another two minutes.

3. Add the "rice" and stir-fry for three minutes.

4. Add the spices and garlic.

5. Stir-fry for another five minutes, until all ingredients are very hot.

curried vegetable couscous

An aromatic combination of spices makes this Moroccan main classic healthy as well as satisfying! Try different color peppers to add color to this dish!

| prep time 15 m | calories 335 | sodium 37 mg | dietary fiber 16.2 g |
| serves 2 | total fat 7.4 g | total carbs 54.1 g | protein 16.7 g |

method

1. Heat the olive oil in a medium skillet. Sauté the garlic, onion and spices until the onion is translucent.

2. Add the vegetables and the chickpeas and sauté for another five minutes.

3. Add the "couscous" and cover.

4. Turn off the heat and let sit to combine flavors.

5. Fluff with a fork before serving.

ingredients

"COUSCOUS"

½ cup cauliflower heads processed into "couscous" size bits

MAIN INGREDIENTS

1 tsp. olive oil

1 green onion, sliced (green tops included)

½ Bell pepper, diced

1 small yellow squash, diced

1 ripe Roma tomato, chopped

¾ cup canned chickpeas (rinse and drain to remove salty liquid)

1 clove garlic, minced

1 tsp. curry powder

¼ tsp. ginger

¼ tsp. cumin

¼ tsp. cinnamon

¼ tsp. cayenne pepper (leave out if using Madras-style curry powder)

potato-veggie latkes

Chances are you love latkes (who doesn't?) but hardly ever make them because it's so time-consuming to grate the potatoes and other vegetables. With a Paderno or Veggetti, that's in the past and there will be a lot more latkes in your future.

prep time 20 m	calories 214	sodium 80 mg	dietary fiber 3.6 g
serves 6	total fat 4.0 g	total carbs 40.5 g	protein 6.4 g

ingredients

4 large baking potatoes, scrubbed and peeled

1 large carrot

1 large yellow onion, grated

2 eggs, beaten

3 Tbsp. matzo meal (or Panko breadcrumbs)

Dash kosher salt

Dash black pepper

Vegetable oil for frying

method

1. Use your spiralizer to shred the potatoes and carrot.

2. Combine in with the grated onion in a colander set over a large bowl. Press down with the back of a spoon to squeeze as much moisture as possible out of the mixture.

3. Let drain for five minutes.

4. Discard the liquid, then combine the vegetables with the eggs and matzo meal.

5. Add ground pepper and salt.

6. Coat the bottom of a heavy-duty skillet (cast-iron is perfect) with oil.

7. Drop spoonfuls of the batter into the oil and flatten with the back of a spoon or spatula.

8. Fry the latkes until they are golden brown on one side, then flip them over to brown on the other side.

9. Drain on a baking sheet that's been lined with paper towels.

10. Serve hot with sour cream and apple sauce.

Note: If you are trying to limit your intake of simple carbs, it's easy to make these vegetable fritters out of quality-carb veggies like zucchini and other squash instead of potatoes.

mediterranean squash stir-fry

This side dish can be customized in multiple ways. Slice the squash and tomatoes into rounds for a pleasing presentation, substitute green tomatoes for a tangy variation.

prep time 10 m	calories 331	sodium 95 mg	dietary fiber 12.0 g
serves 2	total fat 17.9 g	total carbs 40.6 g	protein 11.8 g

method

1. Wash the squash and cut off the blossom end of the zucchini. Use the thick-strand option to make your squash "spaghetti."

2. Put the oil and 2 Tbsp. water in a medium skillet.

3. Combine the "pasta" and MAIN INGREDIENTS in the skillet and cook on medium until the vegetables are soft but not mushy.

4. Sprinkle with the Italian seasoning and cook another minute or so to blend the flavors.

5. If necessary, add another tablespoon or two of water.

6. Sprinkle with parmesan cheese and serve immediately or at room temperature.

ingredients

"PASTA"

3 large zucchini

2 large yellow squash

MAIN INGREDIENTS

1 large yellow onion

2 ripe tomatoes, diced or cut into rounds

2 large garlic cloves, minced

1 Tbsp. Italian seasoning

2 Tbsp. Olive oil

4 Tbsp. water (as needed)

Parmesan cheese

veggeroni & cheese

Everybody's favorite comfort food without the gluten or carbs and with an extra boost of green vegetables! Make it quickly on the stove top or bake it to a crispy goodness.

prep time 15–60 m   calories 343   sodium 360 mg   dietary fiber 2.3 g

serves 4–6   total fat 22.5 g   total carbs 19.1 g   protein 18.8 g

ingredients

"VEGGERONI"

4-6 zucchini or four large broccoli stalks

MAIN INGREDIENTS

2 Tbsp. unsalted butter or olive oil

4 Tbsp. gluten-free flour

4 cups milk (can use non-fat)

1 9-ounce package of Cheddar cheese, grated

method

1. Using spiralizer, create 4 cups of vegetable noodles and set aside.

2. In a heavy duty saucepan, melt the butter (or heat the olive oil).

3. Add the gluten-free flour and mix to make a "roux."

4. Add the milk and whisk until the milk begins to thicken into a sauce.

5. Add the grated cheese and stir until it melts.

6. Add the veggie noodles and heat through, about five minutes.

Serve hot right off the stove, or bake in a greased glass pan at 350 degrees until the cheese gets a little crusty on top (about 45 minutes).

Note: If you've ever used spinach- or tomato-flavored pasta to make Mac n Cheese, you know that kids really like the idea of "green" noodles. Encourage that fascination!

cabbage and apple sauté

This hearty side dish has its roots in pioneer days when cabbages were the only fresh vegetable available and dried apples the only fruit. This savory sauté would be right at home on a Thanksgiving table.

prep time 30 m	calories 413	sodium 1318 mg	dietary fiber 3.6 g
serves 4	total fat 23.7 g	total carbs 26.4 g	protein 21.6 g

method

1. Fry the bacon in a heavy skillet. Drain bacon and set aside.

2. Reserve 2 Tbsp. bacon fat in the skillet.

3. Shred the cabbage.

4. Place the chopped onion in the skillet.

5. Stir to coat with the bacon fat and then sauté over medium heat until the onion is translucent.

6. Add the cabbage and the bay leaf.

7. Cover and reduce heat.

8. Simmer for 20-30 minutes until the cabbage is tender but still a bit crisp.

9. While simmering the cabbage, spiralize the apples into ribbons. Squeeze 1-2 Tbsp. of fresh lemon juice over the apple spirals, and set aside.

10. When the cabbage is ready, remove bay leaf, and mix in the apple noodles.

11. Place the hot mixture in dish and garnish with bacon.

12. There's no need to add salt to this dish; the bacon fat will supply plenty of sodium.

Note: Never pour bacon fat down the sink. It clogs your (and your community's) pipes!

ingredients

"RIBBONS"

2 tart apples

MAIN INGREDIENTS

½ pound bacon

1 medium cabbage head

1 large yellow onion, coarsely chopped

1 cup water

1-2 Tbsp. lemon juice

1 small bay leaf

Freshly ground pepper

pasta arrabiata

This extremely simple sauce is deceptively spicy (and you can kick the heat up a notch by just adding more crushed red pepper).

prep time 60 m	calories 103	sodium 11 mg	dietary fiber 2.8 g
serves 4	total fat 7.6 g	total carbs 9.3 g	protein 2.1 g

ingredients

"PASTA"

4 cups zucchini vegetable pasta, uncooked

MAIN INGREDIENTS

2 large cans (28-ounce) diced tomatoes (don't drain)

4 large garlic cloves, minced

1 bunch fresh basil, chopped (1/3-1/2 cup)

2 tsp. crushed red pepper flakes

2 Tbsp. olive oil

method

1. Combine all the ingredients except the basil and the "pasta" in a large saucepan.

2. Simmer for a half-hour to 45 minutes.

3. Add the basil and simmer for another 10 minutes.

4. While the sauce is on its final simmer, warm the pasta by cooking it for three minutes in a pot of boiling water.

5. Serve immediately, garnished with Parmesan cheese and more pepper flakes if desired.

pineapple pasta with minted berry sauce

This surprisingly sophisticated combination of fruits sparked with fresh mint works as both a refreshing end to a dinner party or as a kid-friendly treat in place of ice cream.

prep time 10 m	calories 95	sodium 2 mg	dietary fiber 3.9 g
serves 6–10	total fat 0.2 g	total carbs 24.2 g	protein 0.8 g

method

1. Use the spiralizer's thin blade to create flat "ribbons" of the pineapple. Place in a colander set over a bowl to drain.

2. Combine the thawed raspberries and the chopped mint in a blender or food processor until smooth. (If the sauce is meant to be served to adults, you can spike it with a bit of crème de menthe liqueur.)

3. Divide the "pasta" into serving dishes and pour the sauce over the fruit ribbons.

Note: This fruity dessert can be made even simpler by simply pouring fresh blueberries on top of the pineapple.

ingredients

"PASTA"

1 medium, slightly unripe pineapple

MAIN INGREDIENTS

1 pkg. frozen raspberries

1 bunch mint, chopped

apple ribbon pie with nut crust

Gluten-free living means finding alternatives to traditional baked goods. No one will feel deprived by this yummy dessert with its buttery nut crust. Bonus! Using a spiralizer simplifies the prep.

| prep time 60 m | calories 333 | sodium 30 mg | dietary fiber 5.5 g |
| serves 1–10 | total fat 17.6 g | total carbs 44.2 g | protein 5.0 g |

ingredients

CRUST

2 cups chopped unsalted nuts (walnuts, peanuts, almonds, pecans)

3 Tbsp. melted unsalted butter (do not use margarine)

1 tablespoon granulated sugar

FILLING

6 medium apples, preferably Braeburn (Red and Golden Delicious will get too mushy)

¾ cup granulated sugar

1 tsp. cinnamon

2 Tbsp. rice starch

1 Tbsp. lemon juice

½ cup golden raisins (optional)

method

CRUST

1. Combine ingredients and press into a 9-inch pie pan.

2. Bake at 350 for 10-12 minutes until crunchy but be careful not to burn the nuts.

3. Set crust aside to cool but leave the oven on.

FILLING

1. Preheat oven to 350 degrees.

2. Peel and core the apples and use your spiralizer to slice them into ribbons.

3. Combine the sugar, rice starch, and the cinnamon and mix with the apple ribbons and raisins if desired.

4. Pour into the pie shell.

5. Bake at 400 degrees for 45 minutes to an hour. Filling will be bubbly and a little caramelized.

Note: You can make lovely ribbons out of any firm fruit, so if you like, substitute pears for the apples and add 2 tsp. of ginger to the spice mix.

Chapter 5

PALEO RECIPES

In a nutshell the Paleo Diet (aka "the Caveman Diet") focuses on foods that were only available to our caveman ancestors. That means no grains (cavemen were hunters, not farmers) and no dairy. The Paleo Diet also eliminates most sweeteners (some hard-core Paleo enthusiasts avoid both honey and maple sugar, even though they're available in nature) and all processed foods, including condiments like soy sauce and mustard, and fats that are not plant-based.

The core of the diet is high-quality protein, fresh, non-starchy vegetables, and fruit which makes it easy to include on both gluten-free diets and weight-loss programs. Nuts (except for peanuts, which are actually legumes) and seeds are an integral part of the Paleo Diet, but should be eaten in small quantities if on a weight-loss regimen.

cabbage "spaghetti" with beef sauce

This fusion of classic spaghetti and meatballs and the equally classic cabbage roll is filled with assertive flavors and contrasting textures.

prep time 30 m	calories 426	sodium 226 mg	dietary fiber 7.3 g
serves 4	total fat 21.7 g	total carbs 19.4 g	protein 40.0 g

method

1. Using your spiralizer, shred the cabbage, then sauté it in a large skillet with the oil and water until the cabbage is translucent.

2. Using your spiralizer, create cauliflower "rice" by slicing the heads. If you want a smaller "grain", then pulse the "rice" in a food processor. Cook the cauliflower rice in boiling water for five minutes or until soft. Remove from heat and drain.

3. Fry the ground beef and the diced onion.

4. Heat the olive oil in a large saucepan and add the onion and the garlic, and cook until the onion is translucent.

5. Add the tomatoes, the thyme, paprika, vinegar and the diced tomatoes.

6. Stir and continue cooking until the sauce is thickened, about 10 minutes.

7. Stir in the ground beef and the remaining olive oil.

8. Add the "rice" to the mixture and heat through.

9. Pour the meat mixture over the sautéed cabbage "spaghetti."

Note: For an additional layer of flavor, try smoky Hungarian paprika instead of sweet paprika.

ingredients

"SPAGHETTI"

1 medium head cabbage, cored and shredded

1 Tbsp. olive oil

1 cup water

"RICE"

¾ cup cauliflower

SAUCE

1 pound ground beef

1 yellow onion, diced

2 garlic cloves, minced

3 Tbsp. olive oil

1 medium can (15-ounce) diced tomatoes

3 Tbsp. low-sodium beef stock

2 Tbsp. apple cider vinegar

1 tsp. thyme

2 tsp. paprika

chicken curry with cauliflower "rice"

This version of the Indian staple is made with Paleo-friendly coconut milk instead of dairy and the result is just as dreamy-creamy.

prep time 30 m	calories 440	sodium 141 mg	dietary fiber 5.6 g
serves 4	total fat 26.7 g	total carbs 15.0 g	protein 37.0 g

ingredients

"RICE"

4 cups Cauliflower "rice"

CURRY

1 pound skinless chicken breasts or turkey cutlets

1 cup coconut milk

1 large yellow onion, diced

2 garlic cloves, minced

1 tablespoon olive oil

2 tsp. tomato paste (no sugar)

3 tsp. curry powder

1 tsp. cumin

1 tsp. turmeric

1 tsp. ginger

¼ tsp. cinnamon

method

1. In a heavy pan or wok, sauté the onion and garlic in the olive oil until the onion is translucent.

2. Add all the spices and cook through. (The mixture will be a lovely golden color.)

3. Add the chicken and cook until the chicken pieces are almost completely cooked through.

4. Add the tomato paste and stir well.

5. Add the coconut milk and continue to cook—stirring frequently—until the chicken is completely cooked and the sauce has thickened.

6. Spiralize and process the cauliflower heads to make "rice." Cook or warm the "rice" to taste.

7. Spoon the chicken and sauce over the Cauliflower rice.

Serve immediately.

Note: The basic chrome-yellow curry powder you can buy anywhere is fine for this dish but if you like a little extra heat, use a Madras-style curry blend, or add a teaspoon of cayenne pepper to the basic blend.

paleo chili cincinnati style

Cincinnati chili is often enhanced by sweet spices like cinnamon and cloves or even added chocolate. This recipe makes a chunkier, con carne style that can be eaten alone as well as in the Cincinnati style over noodles.

prep time 20 m	calories 368	sodium 668 mg	dietary fiber 5.8 g
serves 6–8	total fat 13.9 g	total carbs 17.3 g	protein 44.7 g

method

1. Brown the beef and the sausage in a large skillet with the coconut oil.

2. Drain the meat and put into a large saucepan.

3. Add the chopped vegetables.

4. Add the chili, cumin, paprika, salt, and pepper.

5. Cover and cook for four-six hours over medium heat, stirring occasionally.

6. If the mixture gets too thick, add water, ½ cup at a time.

7. Spiralize the zucchini into noodles. When ready to serve, toss the noodles into a pot of boiling water for 3-5 minutes (long enough to heat through without losing their al dente identity).

8. Ladle chili over warmed "noodles" to serve.

Note: The chili can be prepared in a slow cooker.

ingredients

"NOODLES"

2 zucchini per serving, spiralized into noodles

CHILI

2 pounds lean ground beef

1 pound ground turkey sausage

4 pounds tomatoes, washed, de-seeded and chopped

1 large yellow onion, chopped

1 green bell pepper, chopped

1 jalapeno pepper, diced

2-3 large garlic cloves, minced or crushed

4 Tbsp. chili powder

2 Tbsp. cumin

1 Tbsp. coconut oil

2 tsp. paprika

1 tsp. salt

1 tsp. ground black pepper

curried leek & lentil soup

Hardcore followers of the Paleo diet do not allow lentils on their menu as they are edible pulses that have been cultivated since the Neolithic era (roughly 13,000 years ago). At the same time, though, many who follow the "Caveman" diet make exceptions for dark chocolate, which is also post-Paleolithic, although it has been cultivated for 3,000 years. If you don't want to stray outside the lines, simply leave out the lentils and turn this into a lovely, curry-scented broth with vegetables.

prep time 30–45 m	calories 122	sodium 25 mg	dietary fiber 7.4 g
serves 8–10	total fat 1.9 g	total carbs 18.6 g	protein 5.8 g

ingredients

SPIRALIZED VEGGIES

3 large carrots, sliced into "coins"

2 large leeks (white parts only), cut into ribbons

MAIN INGREDIENTS

1 Tbsp. olive oil

1 yellow onion, coarsely chopped

5 cloves garlic, minced

¼ tsp ginger (1 Tbsp. if fresh grated)

2 Tbsp. curry powder

1 tsp. cumin

1 cup green lentils, rinsed (optional)

6 cups water

method

1. In a large soup pot, sauté the onion in the olive oil over medium heat until translucent.

2. Spiralize the leeks into ribbons, and slice the carrots into coins. Add them to the soup pot.

3. Sauté until the leeks are tender. (Carrots will still be slightly firm.)

4. Add the spices and stir so the vegetables are evenly coated.

5. Add the lentils and the water.

6. Cover the pot and bring to a boil.

7. Reduce heat and simmer for 10-15 minutes to blend flavors. If using lentils, simmer for 25-30 minutes until lentils are tender, stirring occasionally.

iceberg fajitas

While this recipe does not require a spiralizer to make, it's worth trying because it's simply delicious! Substitute crisp iceberg lettuce leaves for corn or flour tortillas and you've got a Paleo version of this classic Mexican dish.

prep time 30 m	calories 262	sodium 135 mg	dietary fiber 2.2 g
serves 4	total fat 10.0 g	total carbs 7.9 g	protein 33.8 g

method

1. Combine 1 Tbsp. of the oil and the spices in a large Ziplock bag and add the uncooked chicken. Toss until the meat is coated with the spice mixture.

2. Heat the remaining oil in a large skillet and add the prepared chicken pieces.

3. When the chicken pieces are nearly cooked through (white with pink centers), add the julienned vegetables.

4. Sprinkle with the lime juice.

5. Remove from heat when the chicken is completely cooked.

6. Divide fajitas into four portions and serve wrapped in a lettuce leaf.

ingredients

4 large lettuce leaves

1 pound boneless, skinless chicken breasts, cut into strips

3 Tbsp. coconut or olive oil

1 large yellow onion, julienned

1 large green pepper, seeded and julienned

Juice of one large lime

1 large garlic clove, minced

1 tsp. chili powder

1 tsp. cumin

pumpkin pasta with bacon & greens

This is a variation of one of the simplest and most decadent pasta dishes ever invented. The pumpkin pairs exceptionally well with the smoky bacon, but you can use any veggie pasta you like.

prep time 20 m	calories 321	sodium 1344 mg	dietary fiber 1.1 g
serves 4–8	total fat 24.0 g	total carbs 3.2 g	protein 22.4 g

ingredients

"PASTA"

4 cups pumpkin pasta, warmed

SAUCE

1 pound bacon

4 large garlic cloves, chopped

1 bunch spinach, shredded

1 Tbsp. dried red pepper flakes (or to taste)

method

1. Fry the bacon until crisp. Remove from heat and put aside to cool.

2. Saute the chopped garlic in the remaining bacon fat until it is golden brown.

3. Add the dried pepper flakes.

4. Spiralize the pumpkin into nice pasta ribbons. Warm them (saute, blanche, nuke, or boil).

5. Combine the warmed pasta and the shredded spinach.

6. Pour the bacon mixture over the pasta and spinach and mix well.

7. Serve immediately.

Note: The combination of hot bacon fat and spinach will remind diners of classic "wilted salads," while the nuttiness of the garlic and the heat of the pepper will cut the richness of the bacon fat.

mexican tomato soup with squash noodles

Mexican cooking is more than just corn tortillas and melted cheese. If you have time, you can make this with fresh tomatoes, but canned tomatoes work just as well.

| prep time 30 m | calories 128 | sodium 141 mg | dietary fiber 4.6 g |
| serves 6 | total fat 9.0 g | total carbs 11.0 g | protein 2.4 g |

method

1. In a heavy soup pot or Dutch oven, sauté the onion and garlic in the olive oil until the onion is translucent.

2. Add the crushed tomatoes and water.

3. Stir in the spices and diced chiles.

4. Bring to a boil, reduce heat and simmer for 15 minutes.

5. Use your spiralizer to slice the squash into noodles.

6. Return to a boil and add the squash noodles. Cook for 8 minutes, or until the vegetable noodles are "done."

7. Serve hot, garnished with roasted pumpkin seeds, a bit of chopped cilantro and cubes of ripe avocado.

Note: Not everyone loves cilantro, so if serving this soup to guests, consider passing the garnishes around the table rather than adding them before the soup is served.

ingredients

"NOODLES"

Two cups yellow or butternut squash

SOUP

1 large can crushed tomatoes

3 quarts water

1 Tbsp. olive oil

1 large yellow onion, coarsely chopped

1 small can diced green chiles, drained

2 garlic cloves, minced

1 tsp. cumin

Roasted pumpkin seeds (pepitas)

1 ripe avocado, cubed

1 bunch cilantro, chopped

beef paprikash with squash noodles

Also known as "beef goulash," this recipe is often made with the addition of sour cream, but the real heart of the flavor is the interaction of meat and paprika, and this version of a comfort food classic (served on a bed of squash noodles) is totally Paleo-friendly.

prep time 3 h	calories 572	sodium 817 mg	dietary fiber 17.7 g
serves 2	total fat 25.4 g	total carbs 53.0 g	protein 40.7 g

ingredients

"NOODLES"

4 cups thick-cut squash

PAPRIKASH

½ lb. stew beef, cut into cubes

2 cups beef broth

2 Tbsp. olive oil

8 Roma tomatoes, seeded and diced

2 large yellow onions, diced

1 green bell pepper, seeded and diced

2 cups beef broth

2 large garlic cloves, minced

3 Tbsp. paprika (or to taste)

2 tsp. caraway seeds

method

1. Preheat oven to 350.

2. Sear the beef cubes in the olive oil in the bottom of a Dutch oven. Push the beef cubes to the side and Saute the onions, bell pepper, and garlic, cooking until the onions are translucent.

3. Add the tomatoes and beef stock.

4. Roast at 350 for 2-2 ½ hours until the beef is tender is so tender it can be shredded with a fork.

5. Using your Veggetti or Paderno spiralizer, slice the squash into thick-cut noodles. Place the noodles into boiling water for a couple minutes, just enough to warm them.

6. Serve the paprikash over warmed "noodles."

Note: This can be made in a crockpot.

rosemary root vegetable soup

You've probably had potatoes roasted with olive oil and rosemary; this soup is basically constructed using the same foundation.

prep time 20 m	calories 167	sodium 89 mg	dietary fiber 6.1 g
serves 6	total fat 6.0 g	total carbs 23.4 g	protein 6.5 g

method

1. Prepare ribbons by spiralizing the parsnips, carrots and beets.

2. Heat the onions in the bottom of a heavy soup pot or Dutch oven until they are translucent.

3. Add the herbs.

4. Add the broth and water and bring to a boil.

5. Add the vegetable ribbons and reduce heat.

6. Simmer until the "pasta" ribbons are al dente.

Note: For additional flavor, use bacon fat instead of the olive oil. You can also substitute 1 ½ tablespoons of Herbes de Provence for the rosemary, thyme, and oregano.

ingredients

"RIBBONS"

3 large parsnips

3 large carrots

3 large beets

SOUP

1 large yellow onion, sliced

1 quart beef or bone broth

2 quarts water

2 Tbsp. olive oil

1 Tbsp. rosemary

1 tsp. thyme

1 tsp. oregano

pesto zucchini pasta with sausage

Pesto sauce is traditionally made with pine nuts, but this recipe uses walnuts.

| prep time 15 m | calories 390 | sodium 313 mg | dietary fiber 4.6 g |
| serves 2–3 | total fat 34.2 g | total carbs 12.6 g | protein 14.3 g |

ingredients

"PASTA"

3 Zucchini

SAUCE

1 pkg. hot Italian turkey sausage

1 cup fresh basil

½-3/4 cup walnut pieces

4 large garlic cloves, minced

1 green bell pepper, seeded and diced

4 Tbsp. olive oil

Dash salt

method

1. Chop the sausages into bite-size pieces and brown in a non-stick pan. Set aside.

2. Combine all the other ingredients in the bowl of a food processor and blend until smooth.

3. Slice the zucchini into pasta ribbons using your spiralizer.

4. Warm the zucchini pasta in boiling water, drain, and put in a large bowl.

5. Toss with the pesto sauce and cooked pieces of sausage.

Serve immediately.

Note: Chunks of skinless chicken breast can be substituted for the sausage.

Chapter 6

WEIGHT LOSS RECIPES

You can dress it up or down, but in the end, losing weight comes down to math: you have to use up more calories than you take in. You can do this one of two ways. Either eat fewer calories or get more exercise. The key is not necessarily eating less, just eating better. Chances are, if you're a serial dieter, you've tried all sorts of eating plans. You may even have lost weight. But chances are your resolve only lasted until your next encounter with a trigger food because your diet left you hungry.

That's where vegetables come in. All foods are not created equal when it comes to calories and vegetables are packed with satisfying fiber while delivering minimal calories. In other words, nutrition-dense vegetables will fill you up but not weigh you down. And bonus! When you substitute more vegetables for fattening fare like pasta and potatoes, your digestive system works more efficiently.

A special note about salt: The recipes in this section contain no added salt. Being overweight puts individuals at risk for hypertension (high blood pressure) and heart disease and a high sodium intake can increase that risk. You will find that as you decrease the salt in your diet you will come to appreciate the natural flavors of your food more. You may also find that extremely salty foods (chips, olives) no longer seem as tasty.

beet salad

This colorful, naturally sweet salad is eaten raw, unlike many roasted beet salads, which makes it easy to prepare.

prep time 5–10 m	calories 315	sodium 117 mg	dietary fiber 3.5 g
serves 2	total fat 28.5 g	total carbs 16.4 g	protein 2.7 g

method

1. Wash and peel the beets, slice into beautiful ribbons using your spiralizer.

2. Combine the rest of the ingredients and pour over the beets.

3. Toss to coat.

4. Serve immediately.

Note: You can make this with red beets alone, but in the spring, when baby golden beets are available, they make a colorful addition. Try substituting orange juice for the vinegar.

ingredients

"RIBBONS"

3 beets (about half a pound)

DRESSING

2 Tbsp. balsamic vinegar

4 Tbsp. olive oil

1 large garlic clove, minced

2 tsp. minced rosemary

south of the border jicama salad

Jicama (also known as the "Mexican turnip") has a taste and texture reminiscent of a crisp apple or raw potato, and its mild taste makes it a versatile addition to all kinds of salads. Here the vegetable takes center stage with a spicy dressing that replicates the flavors of a popular street snack—jicama slices sprinkled with chili powder and lime juice.

prep time 5–10 m	calories 477	sodium 34 mg	dietary fiber 32.7 g
serves 2	total fat 25.9 g	total carbs 60.9 g	protein 5.0 g

ingredients

"RIBBONS"

2 medium jicama (about the size of a yellow onion)

DRESSING

3 limes, juiced (about ¼ cup)

1/4 cup olive oil (four tsp.)

½ tsp. chili powder

1 large garlic clove, minced

Dash red pepper flakes (optional)

method

1. Remove the jicama's papery outer "skin" and slice using the "thick-strand" option on your Veggetti or Paderno slicer.

2. Set aside in a medium bowl.

3. Combine other ingredients and pour over jicama.

4. Toss to mix the dressing evenly.

5. Serve immediately.

Note: Jicama is also used a lot in Asian cooking and you can give an "Asian-fusion" flavor to the salad by adding a dash of low-sodium soy sauce to the dressing along with a tsp. of Chinese five-spice powder.

chicken "noodle" soup

The virtues of chicken soup have been celebrated in nearly every culture, and for good reason. This is a home-made version that "cheats" a little bit by using chicken broth as a base, but it sacrifices nothing in nutrition.

prep time 15 m	calories 170	sodium 156 mg	dietary fiber 3.9 g
serves 2–4	total fat 6.7 g	total carbs 13.3 g	protein 14.5 g

method

1. Combine the chicken broth, water, garlic, onion, curry powder, and olive oil in a medium saucepan and bring to a boil.

2. Reduce heat to a simmer and cover.

3. In a non-stick pan, sauté the diced chicken pieces until they're white all the way through. (Be careful not to overcook the chicken.).

4. Use your spiralizer to make pasta spirals out of the carrots and broccoli.

5. Add the chicken and the vegetable noodles to the simmering soup.

6. Garnish with a dash of pepper flakes.

7. Simmer briefly until all the ingredients are heated through, about two minutes.

Note: Broccoli stem pasta strands taste great but don't "present" as well as other vegetable-based pastas. You can substitute zucchini or any other squash strands in this dish.

ingredients

"NOODLES"

2 large carrots

2 big bunches of broccoli (stems only, save the florets for another use)

SOUP

4 cups (1 quart) low sodium chicken broth

8 cups water

2-3 skinless chicken breasts, diced

1 large onion, diced

2 minced garlic cloves

1 Tbsp. olive oil

2 Tbsp. curry powder

Dash red pepper flakes

zucchini pasta ala checca

This no-cook variation of an Italian classic is gluten-free, vegan/vegetarian, low-cholesterol, low calorie, and kid-friendly.

prep time 15 m	calories 340	sodium 311 mg	dietary fiber 7.9 g
serves 2	total fat 13.4 g	total carbs 26.6 g	protein 28.9 g

ingredients

"PASTA"

4 large zucchini

SAUCE

6 large ripe Roma tomatoes, diced

6-8 fresh basil leaves roughly chopped

4 green onions, diced (white parts only)

2 large garlic cloves, minced

1 Tbsp. grated Parmesan cheese

¼ cup olive oil

Freshly ground pepper

method

1. Combine all the ingredients except the zucchini in a glass or ceramic bowl. Cover and allow to stand at room temperature for two hours to blend flavors. (Refrigerate if you won't use it right away, just bring the mixture to room temperature before mixing with the warm Veggetti.)

2. Make "pasta" strands out of zucchini with your spiralizer.

3. Warm the strands by quickly dunking them in a pot of boiling water.

4. Drain pasta and top with room-temperature sauce.

5. Toss to distribute the sauce evenly throughout the pasta.

6. Serve immediately.

Note: Parmesan cheese is extremely salty, but 1 tablespoon divided among two servings is not a lot, especially if you don't add any additional salt. The trick to staying on any kind of eating plan is making the food palatable.

chicken veggie alfredo

*The classic pasta dish reimagined as a luxurious, low-carb, gluten-free dish. Best of all,
it's a satisfying combination of protein and high-quality dairy along with the vegetables.
That's a win/win/win.*

prep time 20 m	calories 274	sodium 190 mg	dietary fiber 2.3 g
serves 2-4	total fat 11.1 g	total carbs 16.6 g	protein 27.6 g

method

1. Start with the chicken pieces at room temperature.

2. Use your spiralizer to make pasta strands of the zucchini or broccoli and set aside.

3. Bring a pot of water to a boil.

4. Heat the olive oil in a large saucepan. Sauté the minced garlic for about a minute. Add the starch and stir to combine. Cook another two minutes, stirring occasionally over medium heat.

5. Pour the chicken broth into the garlic mixture slowly. Use a whisk to beat the mixture until it's smooth. Add the milk and whisk until smooth and thickened. Simmer for another minute, then add the cheese, stirring constantly until it's melted.

6. Add the fresh pepper and stir one more time. Turn off the heat.

7. Boil the vegetable pasta strands for 2-3 minutes. Drain and put into a large bowl.

8. Add the chicken pieces and then pour the sauce over everything.

9. Toss to combine and serve immediately.

Note: You can serve this as a vegetarian entrée, substituting vegetable broth or water for the chicken broth. You can also add a handful of frozen (defrosted) peas to the mixture for a little extra color.

ingredients

"PASTA"

4-6 zucchini (or 4 broccoli stalks)

ALFREDO

2 chicken breasts without skin, lightly sautéed in olive oil, then cut into pieces

1 cup low-sodium chicken broth

1 cup low-fat milk (don't use no-fat)

1 Tbsp. olive oil

1 cup freshly grated Parmesan cheese (don't use dried Parmesan)

4 garlic cloves, minced (or 2 teaspoons prepared minced garlic)

3 Tbsp. cornstarch (preferred, but you can also use rice starch or flour)

Freshly ground black pepper

pasta primavera salad

This all-veggie variation on the carb-laden dish is high on eye-appeal and delivers bonus nutrition in every bite. Use a combination of yellow and Italian squash for the pasta to make it even more colorful.

| prep time 15 m | calories 310 | sodium 50 mg | dietary fiber 5.1 g |
| serves 4 | total fat 26.9 g | total carbs 17.5 g | protein 3.7 g |

ingredients

"PASTA"

4 cups zucchini or yellow squash

SAUCE

1 bell pepper (any color), diced

1 bunch green onions, chopped

6 Roma tomatoes, seeded and diced

2 large carrots, cut into "coins"

½ cup olive oil

½ cup red wine vinegar

1-2 garlic cloves, minced

1 Tbsp. Italian seasoning

Dash black pepper

method

1. Spiralize the zucchini (or yellow squash) into nice veggie pasta.

2. Warm the pasta in a pot of boiling water while prepping the "sauce."

3. Combine chopped vegetables with the warm pasta.

4. Mix olive oil, vinegar, garlic, and Italian seasoning.

5. Add black pepper to taste.

6. Toss pasta to combine ingredients.

7. Garnish with a sprinkle of Parmesan cheese.

Note: This dish can be served hot, at room temperature, or cold as a pasta salad. Add some pieces of cooked chicken to make it an entrée for two.

yellow squash pasta with sun-dried tomatoes

This is a beautiful dish with its yellow pasta and deep red sun-dried tomatoes. If you're in a hurry, you can even make it with a bottled salad dressing, just choose one without sugar (harder than it sounds) to keep the calories down.

prep time 15 m	calories 286	sodium 82 mg	dietary fiber 1.8 g
serves 2-4	total fat 28.0 g	total carbs 7.0 g	protein 4.1 g

method

1. Using your Veggetti or Paderno spiralizer, slice the yellow squash into nice pasta ribbons.

2. Place the cut-up sun-dried tomato strips in a bowl and cover with boiling water to rehydrate them.

3. Warm the veggie pasta for three minutes in boiling water.

4. Combine the oil, vinegar, garlic, and spices. Pour over the warm pasta.

5. Drain the tomato bits and add to the pasta.

6. Sprinkle with the Parmesan cheese and toss to coat.

7. Serve warm or cold as a pasta salad.

Note: There's no need for added salt with this dish as the Parmesan cheese is quite salty.

ingredients

"PASTA"

4 cups yellow squash (4-6 stalks)

SAUCE

1 package sun-dried tomatoes, cut into strips

½ cup Parmesan cheese

½ cup olive oil

2/3 cup red wine vinegar

2-3 garlic cloves, minced

1 Tbsp. Italian seasoning

beef salad

This beef salad is a tasty alternative to Asian-style beef salads that are loaded with sodium due to the soy sauce in them.

prep time 15 m	calories 947	sodium 1137 mg	dietary fiber 6.2 g
serves 2	total fat 83.7 g	total carbs 17.4 g	protein 40.2 g

ingredients

"NOODLES"

1 large head of iceberg lettuce

MAIN INGREDIENTS

½ pound rare roast beef, cut into strips

1 basket grape tomatoes, washed and drained

1 small red onion, thinly sliced

1 large package pre-washed spinach leaves, shredded

2 Tbsp. prepared horseradish (a brand like Trader's Joe's without soy oil or sugar)

¾ cup olive oil

method

1. Using your spiralizer, slice the iceberg lettuce into short "noodles."

2. Combine the beef, the tomatoes, noodles and the shredded spinach.

3. Mix the horseradish and the olive oil and pour over the other ingredients.

4. Toss to mix salad.

5. Serve chilled.

Note: Use any combination of greens you like—romaine is always a good choice and if you must restrict your intake of Vitamin K because you take blood thinners, a good alternative to spinach.

roasted vegetable snacks

Dieters often complain of the lack of satisfying alternatives to high-sodium, high-calorie snack foods. This quick trick turns veggies into great-tasting and low-sodium treats.

prep time 25 m	calories 22	sodium 4 mg	dietary fiber 0.6 g
serves	total fat 1.5 g	total carbs 2.2 g	protein 0.3 g

method

1. Preheat oven to 450 degrees.

2. Use your spiralizer to make strands from your chosen vegetable.

3. Combine the olive oil and spice in a large Ziplock bag.

4. Add the vegetable strands and shake well to coat evenly.

5. Arrange the strands on a baking sheet that has been brushed with olive oil or coated with cooking spray.

6. Roast until crispy.

7. Let cool, then break up. The resulting crunchies will remind you of the crisp noodles that garnish Chinese chicken salad.

Note: Use any combination of spices you want. Garlic and black pepper is also nice.

ingredients

"STRANDS"

1 large butternut squash, peeled (or any vegetable you choose)

SPICES

1 Tbsp. olive oil

1 Tbsp. curry powder

½ tsp. garlic powder

1 tsp. chili powder

"drunken noodles" with chicken (1)

This traditional Thai recipe is usually made with rice noodles, but since broccoli is often added to the dish, using broccoli "noodles" works as a great substitute without changing the underlying flavors.

prep time 20 m	calories 112	sodium 477 mg	dietary fiber 4.4 g
serves 4	total fat 1.2 g	total carbs 21.6 g	protein 8.5 g

ingredients

"NOODLES"
4 cups of broccoli stalks
MAIN INGREDIENTS
2 chicken breasts, cooked and shredded
2 dried red chilis, de-seeded and chopped finely (or to taste)
2 kaffir lime leaves, sliced very thinly
2 shallots, thinly sliced
4 cloves garlic, minced
1 1-inch piece of ginger, grated
4 ripe cherry tomatoes, halved
1 cup bok choy
2 cups bean sprouts
3-5 basil leaves, chopped
½ cup fresh cilantro, chopped
2 Tbsp. lime juice
1 Tbsp. brown sugar
1 Tbsp. rice vinegar (or white vinegar)
1 Tbsp. "fish sauce" (nam pla, available in most large supermarkets)
½ tsp. "yellow bean sauce" (available in Asian markets, substitute soy sauce if necessary)

method

1. Combine the lime juice, brown sugar, vinegar, and sauces to make the stir-fry sauce.

2. Use your spiralizer to make "noodles" from the broccoli stalks.

3. In a wok, heat a few tablespoons of vegetable oil and add the noodles and the rest of the ingredients except the tomatoes, bean sprouts and cilantro.

4. If you don't have any kaffir lime leaves (available at any Asian market), you can substitute a small bay leaf and about a tablespoon of lime zest in a pinch.

5. Stir fry for two minutes, then add the tomatoes, bean sprouts, cilantro, and stir-fry sauce.

6. Stir-fry until everything is heated through.

7. If the dish seems too salty, add a little more lime juice. Garnish with additional cilantro.

"drunken noodles" with chicken (2)

This variation on traditional Drunken Noodles substitutes health food store ingredients for Asian ingredients, adding a delicious twist to the flavors. I highly recommend comparing the two.

prep time 20 m	calories 240	sodium 209 mg	dietary fiber 3.2 g
serves 4	total fat 6.7 g	total carbs 70.1 g	protein 28.3 g

method

1. Combine the lime juice, liquid aminos and pomegranate molasses to make the stir-fry sauce.

2. Use your spiralizer to make "noodles" from the broccoli stalks.

3. In a wok, heat a few tablespoons of vegetable oil and add the noodles and the rest of the ingredients except the tomatoes, bean sprouts and cilantro.

4. Stir fry for two minutes, then add the tomatoes, bean sprouts, cilantro, and stir-fry sauce.

5. Stir-fry until everything is heated through.

6. If the dish seems too salty, add a little more lime juice. Garnish with additional cilantro.

ingredients

"NOODLES"

4 cups of yellow squash

MAIN INGREDIENTS

2 chicken breasts, cooked and shredded

2 fresh cherry peppers, sliced

2 bay leaves, dried

2 shallots, thinly sliced

4 cloves garlic, minced

1 1-inch piece of ginger, grated

4 ripe cherry tomatoes, halved

1 cup bok choy

2 cups bean sprouts

3-5 basil leaves, chopped

½ cup fresh cilantro, chopped

2 Tbsp. lime juice

2-3 Tbsp. Braggs liquid aminos

2-3 Tbsp. Cortas 100% Pomegranate molasses

perfumed noodles with fruit & nuts

This is a gold-toned adaptation of the classic Middle Eastern dish "jeweled rice." Add cooked chicken or lamb to transform it from a side dish into an entrée.

prep time 20 m	calories 418	sodium 418 mg	dietary fiber 6.3 g
serves 4–6	total fat 30.0 g	total carbs 38.9 g	protein 4.9 g

ingredients

4 cups squash noodles, uncooked

2/3 cup dried chopped dried apricots

1/3 cup golden raisins

½ cup dried cherries (or cranberries)

½ cup coconut oil

1 tsp. ground cardamom

1 thread saffron (if desired)

2/3 cup pistachio nuts, shelled and chopped

¼ tsp. ground pepper

method

1. Lightly sauté the chopped nuts in a tablespoon of the coconut oil.

2. Add the fruit and spices.

3. Add the remaining coconut oil and the uncooked squash noodles.

4. Sauté lightly until all the flavors blend.

5. Serve immediately.

6. Note: You can substitute dried pears for the apricots; the result won't be as authentic, but pears pair well with cardamom.

Chapter 7

SOUPS

Noodle soups are universally found throughout the world and are considered comfort food in any language. Starting a meal with a nutritious bowl of soup "takes the edge" off the appetite, and generally results in consuming less calories per meal, a boon for those watching their weight.

GF Gluten-free   V   for Vegetarian
P   Paleo   VG Vegan
WL Weight-Loss

thai chicken noodle soup

This soup features three flavors that define Thai cuisine, coconut, chili, and lime.

| prep time 25–30 m | calories 378 | sodium 1208 mg | dietary fiber 2.4 g |
| serves 4 | total fat 21.6 g | total carbs 17.0 g | protein 30.0 g |

method

1. Combine the chicken broth, jalapeno, garlic, ginger, lime juice and zest and 3 Tbsp. fish sauce in a medium sauce pan and bring to a simmer.

2. Add the noodles and cook for one minute or until tender. Use tongs to remove the noodles. Place in a bowl and cover to keep warm.

3. Add the mushrooms to the simmering broth. Simmer for another four minutes, then add the chicken and the coconut milk.

4. Continue to simmer until the chicken is cooked through.

5. Add the spinach and stir until the leaves get limp, then add the chopped cilantro and remaining tablespoon of fish sauce.

6. Divide the cooked noodles into four bowls and pour the soup over the noodles.

ingredients

GF P WL

½ cup zucchini noodles, spaghetti cut

2 boneless, skinless chicken breasts cut into bite-size pieces

5 cups chicken broth

1 cup coconut milk (can use low-fat)

2 jalapeno peppers, seeded and chopped finely

2 large cloves garlic, chopped

1 ½ inch piece ginger root, grated

1 Tbsp. lime zest

¼ cup fresh lime juice

4 Tbsp. fish sauce (I use Red Boat)

2 cups shiitake mushrooms, sliced

2 cups baby spinach leaves

2 Tbsp. chopped cilantro

tunisian noodle soup

This spicy noodle soup is a vegetarian African variation of the ubiquitous chicken noodle soup.

prep time 25–30 m	calories 181	sodium 184mg	dietary fiber 2.9 g
serves 4-6	total fat 10.0 g	total carbs 20.7 g	protein 4.7 g

GF P WL

ingredients

2 cups zucchini noodles, spaghetti cut

2 quarts vegetable stock (or chicken stock)

1 pound Swiss chard, chopped coarsely (stems, ribs, and eaves)

1 large red onion, chopped

3 large garlic cloves, minced

4 Tbsp. olive oil (or coconut oil)

2 Tbsp. tomato paste

2 Tbsp. hot pepper sauce

1 Tbsp. fresh lemon juice

method

1. Bring the stock to a boil in a stockpot. Add the chard and cook until the chard is wilted.

2. Stir in the tomato paste, oil, hot pepper sauce, garlic, and onion. Return to a boil and then reduce to a simmer.

3. Simmer for 5-10 minutes, then add the noodles. Cook for about 1 minute, or until they are tender.

mexican chicken noodle soup

This spicy, tomato-based soup is another international variation of chicken noodle soup.

prep time 25–30 m	calories 592	sodium 1336 mg	dietary fiber 2.1 g
serves 6	total fat 33.4 g	total carbs 46.5 g	protein 32.3 g

method

1. In a large stock pot, heat the onion, carrots, and garlic in the oil until the onions are translucent.

2. Add the canned tomatoes (juice and all), the chicken stock and the chicken pieces. Bring to a boil and cook until the chicken is cooked through. Remove the chicken from the pot and set aside to cool.

3. Reduce to a simmer and cover. When the chicken is cool, shred it and return it to the pot, along with the noodles, the spices, and the line juice.

4. Continue to simmer for another 30 seconds, then remove from heat.

ingredients

GF P WL

2 cups zucchini noodles, spaghetti circles cut

6 cups chicken stock

2 14-oz. cans roasted tomatoes

4 boneless, skinless chicken breasts

5 large garlic cloves, minced

1 yellow onion, chopped

1 large bunch cilantro, chopped (approximately 1 cup)

1 jalapeno pepper, seeded and minced

2 medium carrots, chopped into "coins"

Juice of 2 limes

2 Tbsp. olive oil

1 tsp. cumin

1 tsp. turmeric

1 tsp. black pepper

miso noodle soup

This light vegetable/noodle broth can serve as a first course or as a light lunch all by itself.

| prep time 25–30 m | calories 159 | sodium 692 mg | dietary fiber 3.9 g |
| serves 6–8 | total fat 6.1 g | total carbs 20.2 g | protein 7.9 g |

GF P WL V VG

ingredients

1 cup zucchini noodles, udon cut

4 carrots, spaghetti cut

3 quarts water

2 leeks, white part only, sliced

1 bunch Swiss chard (or black kale), about ½ pound

4 carrots, cut into chunks

3 cloves garlic, minced

2 green onions, sliced

1 cup edamame (can use frozen)

½ cup miso paste

1 ½ Tbsp. olive oil

method

1. Heat the oil in a large stock pot for 1 minute, then add the leeks and garlic. Cook over medium heat for another 5 minutes, stirring occasionally.

2. Separate the chard leaves from the ribs and stalks and set aside. Chop the ribs and stalks, then add to the leek and garlic mixture. Continue to cook until the chard is tender, 8-10 minutes. Stir occasionally so the vegetables don't stick.

3. Add the water to the pot and bring to a boil. Add the chopped carrots and reduce heat to a simmer. Simmer for 5 minutes or until the carrots are almost soft.

4. Chop the chard leaves and add to the soup along with the edamame. Simmer until the greens wilt, then bring to a boil.

5. Remove 1 cup of boiling water and add it to the miso paste. Add the miso mixture to the soup along with the noodles and return to a boil. As soon as the noodles are tender (about 30-60 seconds), remove from heat and serve. Garnish with sliced green onions.

Note: You can add chopped chicken or pork to this soup for a heartier version, or diced tofu for a more protein-rich vegetarian/vegan option.

beef pho

Considered the national dish of Vietnam, Pho is traditionally made with beef broth, sometimes enriched with oxtail. This is a simplified version that replaced flat rice noodles with veggie pasta.

prep time 25–30 m	calories 283	sodium 2279 mg	dietary fiber 3.2 g
serves 4	total fat 10.1 g	total carbs 10.8 g	protein 35.7 g

method

1. Combine broth, water, and spices in a large stockpot. Bring to a boil over high heat, then cover the pan and reduce the heat. Simmer for half an hour, stirring occasionally.

2. Add the noodles and beef to the pot, return to a boil just long enough to cook the beef, about 1-2 minutes if the beef is sliced very thin. Remove the cinnamon stick, then serve hot with garnishes as desired.

ingredients

(GF) (P) (WL)

2 cups yellow squash noodles, udon cut

8 cups beef broth, preferably low sodium

4 cups water

¾ pound flank steak, very thinly sliced

1 medium yellow onion, sliced

4-6 garlic cloves, minced

1 2-inch piece ginger root, grated

2 whole cloves

1 cinnamon stick

2 Tbsp. fish sauce

For garnish: chopped green onions, thinly sliced jalapeno peppers, chopped cilantro, lime wedges

minestrone

One of the first Italian words a diner learns (right after "spaghetti," is "minestrone." This classic vegetable soup easily fits into any eating plan that embraces veggies.

prep time 6 h	calories 356	sodium 810mg	dietary fiber 24.4 g
serves 4–6	total fat 2.0 g	total carbs 61.7 g	protein 24.5 g

GF WL V

ingredients

1 cup zucchini or yellow squash pasta, spaghetti circles cut

4 cups chicken broth

1 28-oz. can crushed tomatoes

1 15.5-oz. can cannellini beans, drained and rinsed to remove excess salt

1 cup escarole or kale, shredded

2 large carrots, cut into "coins"

2 ribs celery, diced

1 large yellow onion, chopped

3 large garlic cloves, minced

2 tsp. Italian seasoning

Grated Parmesan cheese (optional)

method

1. Combine the broth and the canned tomatoes (juice included) with the carrots, celery, garlic, and onion in a slow cooker. Stir in the Italian seasoning. (If using tomatoes that have "Italian seasoning" don't add more.)

2. Cover and cook on low for 4-6 hours, then add the escarole, and beans. Cover and increase heat. Cook for another 5-10 minutes, until the greens are wilted.

3. Add the noodles and cook another 1-2 minutes. Serve hot, garnished with Parmesan if desired.

Note: Without the Parmesan garnish, this recipe is Paleo; substitute vegetable broth for the chicken broth to make it vegan.

pasta e fagilo

This pasta and bean soup is another hearty, healthy example of "Mediterranean" cuisine. Substitute short, curly zucchini noodles made with the Paderno for the traditional tiny tube-shaped pasta.

prep time 45 m	calories 549		sodium 1046 mg	dietary fiber 24.2 g
serves 8	total fat 11.0 g	total carbs 76.5 g		protein 38.9 g

method

1. Crumble the sausage into the bottom of a large stockpot or Dutch oven and brown over medium heat. Drain off the excess fat and then add the olive oil, garlic, onions, and carrots. Cook until the vegetables are tender (about 4 minutes). Stir occasionally.

2. Add the water, chicken stock, tomato sauce, and diced tomatoes (including juice). Stir in the Italian seasoning and bring to a boil.

3. Drain and rinse the canned beans, then add to the soup. Add the beans to the pot and reduce heat. Simmer for 2-3 minutes, then toss in the noodles and simmer another 1-2 minutes. Serve hot.

ingredients

GF P

1 cup zucchini or yellow squash pasta, flat semicircles cut

1 pound spicy Italian sausage (if using links, remove casing)

4 cups chicken broth

1 cup water

4 carrots, sliced into coins

1 large yellow onion, diced

4 cloves garlic, crushed

1 16-oz. can tomato sauce

1 15-oz. can diced tomatoes

1 15-oz. can kidney beans

1 15-oz can cannellini or navy beans

1 Tbsp. Italian seasoning

sizzling "rice" soup

Substituting cauliflower for the rice in this recipe gives it an extra layer of flavor as well as converting it into a dish that's gluten-free and paleo.

prep time 25–30 m	calories 579	sodium 374 mg	dietary fiber
serves 8	total fat 56.5 g	total carbs 6.0 g	protein 11.8 g

GF P

ingredients

2/3 cup cauliflower, "rice" cut

3 cups chicken broth

¼ cup baby shrimp (can use canned or frozen)

1 boneless, skinless chicken breast cut into bite-sized pieces

2 Tbsp. chopped water chestnuts

¼ cup bamboo shoots

½ cup mushrooms, sliced

½ cup bean sprouts

1 large egg

2 cups canola oil

1 Tbsp. dry sherry

4 Tbsp. cornstarch

method

1. Combine the egg and cornstarch. Add the shrimp and chicken pieces and stir to coat.

2. Heat 1 ½ cups oil in a wok.

3. Add the chicken and shrimp and quickly stir-fry until cooked through. Remove from oil and set aside.

4. In a large saucepan, combine the broth, mushrooms, and bamboo shoots. Bring to a boil.

5. Add the sherry, reduce heat and simmer.

6. Re-heat the soil in the wok and quickly brown the cauliflower "rice." Remove from the oil and drain. Add the "rice" and bean sprouts to the soup and serve immediately.

pumpkin noodle soup

This soup combines rich fall flavors with an ease of preparation that will make it a favorite.

prep time 25 m	calories 150	sodium 645 mg	dietary fiber 6.3 g
serves 6	total fat 6.3 g	total carbs 19.3 g	protein 6.2 g

method

1. Heat the oil in a large saucepot and add the chopped onions. Cook until the onions are translucent, 3-5 minutes. Stir in the spices.

2. Add the pumpkin puree and the vegetable broth. Bring to a boil, then reduce to a simmer.

3. Stir in the brown sugar.

4. Add the pumpkin noodles and summer for another 2-3 minutes.

Note: Leave out the brown sugar to make this soup Paleo-friendly.

ingredients

(GF) (WL) (V) (VG)

4 cups pumpkin or squash noodles, flat cut

5 cups vegetable broth

1 large (29-oz.) can pumpkin puree (not the pumpkin pie filling kind)

1 large yellow onion, diced

2 Tbsp. olive oil

½ Tbsp. brown sugar

2 tsp. sage (or 2 Tbsp. fresh sage, chopped)

1 tsp. cinnamon

¼ tsp. ginger

¼ tsp. cayenne pepper

1/8 tsp. nutmeg

moroccan chicken with olives

If you can't find preserved lemons in your local market (try the olive bar), you can substitute fresh lemon peel.

prep time 45 m	calories 1288	sodium 3086 mg	dietary fiber 6.3 g
serves 4	total fat 96.1 g	total carbs 36.3 g	protein 68.8 g

GF P

ingredients

4 cups zucchini noodles, cooked al dente

2 cups yellow squash noodles, cooked al dente

3 lbs. chicken legs and thighs

3 cups chicken stock

2 preserved lemons (or rind from two fresh lemons)

¾ cup pitted green olives, rinsed

1 small yellow onion, diced

4 Tbsp. coconut oil

1 garlic clove, minced

1 tsp. grated fresh ginger

1 Tbsp. cumin

1 Tbsp. ground coriander

1 tsp, turmeric

2 tsp. paprika

½ tsp. cayenne pepper

¼ tsp. saffron

method

1. Remove pulp from the preserved lemons and cut peel into narrow strips. If using fresh lemons, cut the rind into narrow strips. Set the lemon strips aside.

2. Combine the squash and zucchini noodles in a medium bowl.

3. Melt the coconut oil in a Dutch oven over medium heat. Add the chicken pieces. Season with salt and pepper to taste, then brown on all sides. (Do this in batches if necessary.) Set the browned chicken aside.

4. Add the onions to the fat and cook until translucent and slightly softened. Add all the spices except the saffron and stir.

5. Return the chicken pieces to the pan and turn until they're coated with the oil/spice mixture.

6. Add the chicken stock and the saffron. Stir.

7. Cover and Reduce heat. Simmer for 25 minutes.

8. Add the lemon strips and olives. Cook for another 5-8 minutes, covered, until the chicken is done.

9. Remove the chicken and set aside.

10. Bring the sauce to a boil and cook until it thickens slightly, about 10 minutes.

11. Divide the vegetable noodles among four plates. Top with the hot sauce, then add the chicken.

shrimp soup with bok choy

This seafood soup is half a world away from the tomato-based seafood stews found in the Mediterranean.

prep time 35–45 m	calories 307	sodium 1066 mg	dietary fiber 1.9 g
serves 6–8	total fat 8.3 g	total carbs 27.5 g	protein 30.4 g

method

1. Heat the oil in a large stockpot and add the bok choy, mushrooms, garlic, ginger, and red pepper flakes. Heat on medium for a minute, then add the broth and clam juice. Cover the pot and bring to a boil.

2. Add the shrimp and sliced green onions. Continue to cook for another 2 minutes, or until shrimp are cooked through.

3. Toss in the noodles, remove from heat and let stand 5 minutes before serving.

ingredients

(GF) (P) (WL)

3 cups zucchini pasta, spaghetti cut

1 ½ cups clam juice (or seafood stock)

6 cups chicken stock

2 lbs. raw shrimp, cleaned, shelled, and deveined

1 large bok choy, trimmed and sliced thinly

3 green onions, thinly sliced

1 Tbsp. crushed red pepper flakes

2 Tbsp. grated ginger

3 large garlic cloves, minced

1/3 lb. shiitake mushrooms, sliced

3 Tbsp. canola oil

black bean & noodle soup

This festive and flavorful soup is high-fiber and low-calorie, and makes an excellent starter for a Cinco de Mayo feast or a treat to kick off an ordinary weekend.

prep time 25 m	calories 334	sodium 887 mg	dietary fiber 13.8 g
serves 6	total fat 2.4 g	total carbs 61.5 g	protein 21.0 g

(GF) (WL) (V) (VG)

ingredients

2 cups zucchini or yellow squash noodles, spaghetti cut

2 14-oz. cans vegetable broth

1 16-oz. jar salsa

1 15-oz can black beans, drained and rinsed

2 cups corn kernels (preferably frozen, not canned)

Juice of one lime

1-2 tsp. chili powder

½ tsp. cumin

method

1. Heat the broth to a boil in a medium saucepan.

2. Add the remaining ingredients.

3. Continue to cook for 1-2 minutes, until noodles are tender.

Note: Feel free to garnish with a dollop of sour cream if not following a vegan diet.

Chapter 8

BONUS SECTION: KEEPING A WELL-STOCKED PANTRY

Nothing makes cooking more frustrating than not having all of the ingredients needed to make something truly delicious. This bonus section will help you keep your pantry well-stocked and ready for whatever inspiration comes your way!

The Gluten-Free (GF) Pantry

Gluten is a protein—technically a mix of proteins—found in some cereal grains. People with celiac disease and gluten allergies cannot tolerate gluten and must avoid it at all costs. For the general population, a growing body of research suggests eliminating gluten will help prevent obesity, diabetes, cardiovascular problems, and digestive disorders like "leaky gut syndrome."

There's also persuasive evidence of a connection between gluten allergies and the onset of Alzheimer's and other dementia. (This has been dubbed "grain brain.")

When living gluten-free is a health imperative rather than simply a dietary choice, it's particularly important to read labels. Gluten can lurk in the most unlikely places (in the malt vinegar you've just sprinkled on your fish and chips, for instance) and words like bulgur, spelt, triticale, and malt can all spell trouble.

WHAT TO STOCK:

- Seeds
- Nuts, nut butters, and nut oils
- Peanuts and peanut butters
- Dried beans and lentils
- Dried fruit
- Larabars—advertised as the "original fruit and nut bar," these treats are contain nothing but fruit, nuts, and spices. (Note: these snacks should not be eaten by those on a weight-loss diet or those with blood sugar issues as they are rank very high on the glycemic index.)
- Blue Diamond Nut thins
- Jerky
- Potato Chips
- Corn tortillas
- Oatmeal certified GF
- Rice Chex or other rice-based cold cereal (Glutino has four different options of cold cereal)
- If your local supermarket/health food store does not carry your favorite brand of GF cereal, try one of the mail order sources like Arrowhead Mills or Bob's Red Mill Natural Foods.
- Rice, brown rice, black rice, wild rice
- Quinoa, millet, amaranth
- Cornmeal

For Baking:

- Almond flour
- Coconut flour
- Arrowroot powder
- Cornstarch
- Tapioca starch
- Gluten-free baking mixes
- There are now a variety of excellent gluten-free baking mixes available, like the ones sold by Bob's Red Mill and Pamela's.
- Honey, Maple Syrup, Blue Agave Syrup

Condiments:

- All herbs, dried and fresh.
- Spices and spice blends (curry powder, chili powder) that do not include additives like sugar or salt.
- Dried seaweed sheets and flakes
- GF soy sauce
- Bragg's Liquid aminos
- Coconut aminos (to substitute for soy sauce, which is made from a legume). If you can't find them in your local supermarket, health or whole foods store, they are readily available online.
- Distilled hot pepper sauces (like Tabasco)
- Mustard, ketchup, mayonnaise, relish

In the Fridge:

- Dairy products, including milk, yogurt, sour cream, and cheese
- Almond Milk
- Soy milk
- Coconut milk
- Eggs
- Unprocessed meat (no hotdogs and especially no corn dogs!)
- Frozen vegetables without sauce
- Frozen fruit without added sugar or sauce
- Gluten-free pie crust

BONUS TOOL FOR GLUTEN-FREE DIETERS: A RICE COOKER

A kitchen-sized version of the giant rice pots found in Asian restaurants, this appliance allows a cook to dump in the rice, water, seasonings and other ingredients, set the timer and walk away. The rice comes out perfect every time, with no burnt crust or soupiness.

The Paleo Pantry

The Paleo diet (also dubbed the "Caveman Diet") is built around the simple concept that eating only the foods available to our ancient hunter/gatherer ancestors is the best way to avoid modern health problems like obesity, Type II diabetes, cardiovascular disease, and cancer.

The Paleo diet is an omnivorous eating plan that includes animal protein, fish, fruits, most vegetables (potatoes are forbidden), seeds, nuts, and vegetable-based fats.

The Paleo diet does NOT include dairy, sugar, grains, legumes, alcohol, or processed foods of any kind except those that have been dehydrated, like raisins and other dried fruit.

Some food lists are stricter than others and there's some disagreement over the inclusion or exclusion of honey, maple syrup, chocolate, coffee, vinegar, and wine. Tailor your diet to your needs, and be realistic. If you want a little dark chocolate or a glass or red wine occasionally, it's not going to throw your eating plan into complete disarray. "Moderation in all things" should be the goal.

WHAT TO STOCK:

- Seeds
- Nuts, nut butters, and nut oils
- Remember, peanuts are not nuts, they're legumes; so no peanuts, peanut butter or peanut oil.
- Olive oil
- Coconut oil
- Dried fruit
- Larabars—advertised as the "original fruit and nut bar," these treats are not just Paleo, they're also gluten-free containing fruit, nuts, and spices. (Note: these snacks should not be eaten by those on a weight-loss diet or those with blood sugar issues as they are rank very high on the glycemic index.)
- Jerky, preferably made without sugar.

Condiments:

- All herbs, dried and fresh.
- Spices and spice blends (curry powder, chili powder) that do not include additives like sugar or salt.
- Dried seaweed sheets and flakes
- Distilled pepper sauces like Tabasco
- Coconut aminos (to substitute for soy sauce, which is made from a legume). If you can't find them in your local supermarket, health or whole foods store, they are readily available online.
- Mustard without additives or thickeners. (You can make your own by mixing mustard or wasabi powder with water.)

- Commercial mayonnaise and ketchup are off the Paleo table. You can make mayonnaise from egg yolks and oil, and ketchup created from scratch.

For Baking:

- Almond flour
- Coconut flour
- Arrowroot powder
- Tapioca starch

In the Fridge:

- Coconut Milk
- Almond Milk
- Eggs
- Frozen vegetables without sauce
- Frozen fruit without added sugar or sauce
- Unprocessed meat (no hotdogs and especially no corn dogs!)

- Beef, pork, lamb, and poultry make up the bulk of animal protein consumed today but the options available in grocery stores already goes far beyond those four meat selections. Ethnic markets often have goat in stock. Rabbit is readily available in the freezer section of most large supermarkets, and in large cities, it's easy to find ground buffalo and ostrich (a red meat) as well. Especially during the winter holidays, many stores allow patrons to special order "exotic" turkey alternates like goose, pheasant, and quail.
- All these meats—and even more exotic victuals like alligator and rattlesnake—are available by mail order.

BONUS TOOL FOR PALEO DIETERS: A DEHYDRATOR

Raw foodists have perfected the art of making crackers and "breads" from seeds with a hydrator. Making meat and fish jerky in a dehydrator is an easy and more energy-efficient process than making it an oven.

Weight-Loss Pantry

Being overweight stresses out your body and contributes to increased risk of heart attack, stroke, diabetes, and cancer. If extra weight is coupled with other risk factors, like smoking or excess alcohol consumption, there's a multiplier effect.

There are a number of effective weight-loss eating plans—from low-carb to high-fiber to low fat—but the outcome of any diet is a matter of simple math. You have to expend more calories than you consume. The best way to accomplish your weight-loss goals is to focus on whole foods, nutrition-dense fruits and vegetables, whole grains, healthy dairy, and quality protein. The more processed a food is, the more chemicals it contains, the less likely it is to be nutritious and satisfying. (It's easy to eat a whole bag of potato chips without putting a dent in your appetite but not as easy to eat a bag of fiber-rich carrots.)

No matter which diet plan you choose to attain your weight loss, getting back to basics and eating "clean" is a good place to start.

When you first embark on a weight-loss regimen, it's tempting to stock up on diet this and low-fat that. But if you're filling your pantry with non-fat cookies and diet soda, you're missing the point. It's also tempting to rely on pre-packed diet meals, either the frozen kind or the dehydrated ones that are delivered monthly to your door. Some of these packaged foods are so filled with preservatives that their sell-by date is not for another decade. Stick with real food.

WHAT TO STOCK:

- Seeds
- Nuts, nut butters, and nut oils
- Peanuts and peanut butters
- Seeds and nuts are good for dieters. A handful of nuts (an ounce or so) makes a satisfying snack thanks to the fat. But practice portion control; it's easy to eat a lot of seeds or nuts in a single sitting.
- Dried popcorn (not the microwave kind)
- Dried beans and lentils
- Dried fruit
- Jerky
- Corn tortillas
- Oatmeal
- Brown rice, wild rice, quinoa, millet, amaranth
- Don't use white rice, it ranks 64 on the glycemic index (GI), and even a small portion can spike blood sugar.
- Whole Wheat flour
- Buckwheat flour
- Honey, Maple Syrup, Blue Agave Syrup
- There are a wide variety of artificial sweeteners on the marketplace. It's counter-intuitive, but some research suggests that these substances can trigger everything from bloating and belly fat production to the onset of Type 2 diabetes. It's better to avoid them altogether and use healthier alternatives. If you must use an artificial sweetener, make it a natural one, like Stevia.

- Coconut oil
- Canola oil
- Olive oil
- Sesame oil
- Vinegar—any kind except flavored vinegars with added sugar. Balsamic vinegar is high in sugar, so use it in moderation.
- Stay away from all commercial salad dressings. They are loaded with salt and sugar, often shockingly so. They also tend to have a lot of preservatives added for long shelf-life. Make your own salad dressing.

Condiments:

- All herbs, dried and fresh
- Spices and spice blends (curry powder, chili powder) that do not include additives like sugar or salt
- Dried seaweed sheets and flakes
- Low-sodium soy sauce
- Distilled hot pepper sauces (like Tabasco)
- Mustard
- Most dieters avoid mayonnaise but it's really ketchup that's the worst condiment culprit. Loaded with sugar, salt, added thickeners and preservatives, putting ketchup on your food is like pouring thick syrup over it. Try one of the organic brands at the health food store if you must have ketchup.

In the Fridge:

- Milk, cheese, Greek yogurt
- When it comes to dairy products, "low fat and non-fat" aren't necessarily the best choices for a weight-loss diet. In one oft-quoted study conducted at the University of Tennessee, researchers found that subjects who were fed a diet rich in whole milk lost more belly fat than those given low-fat or no-fat dairy. And while the findings are controversial, other research suggests that the added fat in whole milk actually boosts fat-burning. If you want a glass of whole milk, go ahead, just don't blend it into a milkshake if you want to lose weight.
- Eggs
- Unprocessed meat—stay away from processed meats like bologna, lunch meats, and hot dogs. Bacon can be included in a low-carb regimen, but if possible, choose an uncured, sugar-free, nitrate-free brand. There are a number of mail-order sources for these brands if they are not available in your local area.
- Frozen vegetables without sauce
- Frozen fruit without added sugar or sauce
- Frozen fish without breading

BONUS TOOL FOR GLUTEN-FREE DIETERS: A SLOW COOKER

Slow cookers are larger than crockpots and allow a cook more flexibility. Either appliance is useful for creating stews, soups, spaghetti sauce, and chilis, but the slow-cooker allows for bigger batches at a time, which is a boon for the busy cook. Making food ahead and freezing individual portions means that there's always something good to eat in the length of time it takes to microwave the meal.

A FREE GIFT

Thank you for purchasing this book and reading it to the end! My sincere hope is that you tried several or more recipes, and found them to be every bit as delicious and worthwhile as you had hoped. *(If not, then contact us and let us know! We want these books to be a valuable and meaningful part of your life, so we love comments - good or bad - from our readers.)*

As a way of showing my appreciation, let me give you another recipe book for absolutely free and without obligation. Every month we release a new book to our readers...absolutely free! This helps us get early feedback about the book before launching it to the public. We get feedback, and you get delicious and creative recipes for free!

To receive your free recipe book, just go to this page:
www.HealthyHappyFoodie.org/freebook

Enjoy!

J.S. Amie

ABOUT THE AUTHOR

J.S. Amie is "the Healthy Happy Foodie"—a food blogger and Amazon bestselling author who is quickly building a name as a trusted source for delicious recipes which support healthy diets and lifestyles including Gluten-free and Paleo diets. Her books on vegetable spiralizer recipes are gaining popularity with a wide variety of people who all share the same passion for eating well while staying healthy.

She is a mother of two charming daughters, who, like normal children, crave sugar, wheat and more sugar! So what to do? JS decided to learn how to satisfy those urges by substituting good, natural food for unhealthy junk. Her books reflect her personal mission to nourish her family and friends as well as possible. She lives in a small town surrounded by rolling hills, walnut trees and zombies. Just kidding about the zombies.

She can be contacted on her blog at www.HealthyHappyFoodie.org.

ALSO BY J.S. AMIE

All books are available directly from HealthyHappyFoodie.org, or from reputable online booksellers like Amazon.com or BarnesAndNoble.com.

LEGAL DISCLAIMER

The information contained in this book is the opinion of the author and is based on the author's personal experience and observations. The author does not assume any liability whatsoever for the use of or inability to use any or all information contained in this book, and accepts no responsibility for any loss or damages of any kind that may be incurred by the reader as a result of actions arising from the use of information in this book. Use this information at your own risk.

The author reserves the right to make any changes he or she deems necessary to future versions of the publication to ensure its accuracy.